CW01637352

MY KITCHEN RULES

BEST OF THE BEST COOKBOOK

MKR MY KITCHEN RULES

BEST OF THE BEST COOKBOOK

hachette AUSTRALIA

CONTENTS

APPETISERS, SIDES AND SALADS 1

TURKEY SAN CHOI BOW
with Fried Wonton Skins 3

PHỞ ON THE GO 4

CORN, ZUCCHINI AND HALOUMI FRITTERS
with Smoky Tomato Relish and Avocado Cream 7

GRANDMA'S BRANDY PÂTÉ
with Homemade Brioche and Chutney 9

MUSHROOM SOUP
with Goat's Cheese Croutons 12

BREAKFAST DAMPER
with Tomato Relish 15

SALT AND PEPPER MUD CRAB
with Chilli Soy Dipping Sauce 16

STEAMED OYSTERS
with Vermicelli and XO Sauce, Mushrooms and Chinese Greens 19

AGEDASHI TOFU
with Pork Gyoza 20

SAGANAKI PRAWNS
with Tomato, Feta and Homemade Crusty Bread 23

WARM DUCK SALAD
with Beetroot, Pomegranate and Redcurrant Vinaigrette 24

CRISPY CHICKEN
on Asian Rice Noodle Salad 27

SEARED MOROCCAN TUNA
and Cured Salmon 28

ZESTY PRAWN SALAD 31

VIETNAMESE PORK AND PRAWN PANCAKES 32

BACON HUEVOS RANCHEROS
with Bloody Mary Salsa 35

VIETNAMESE BAGUETTES 36

CHICKEN ADOBO TORTILLAS
with Pomegranate and Lime Salad 39

WAGYU BEEF CARPACCIO 40

SCALLOP CEVICHE 43

GOAT'S CHEESE CROQUETTES
with Rocket and Apple Salad and Caramelised Macadamias 44

BEETROOT TART
with Goat's Cheese Mousse and Balsamic Reduction 47

SINGAPOREAN CHILLI SOFT SHELL CRAB 48

PIZZA WITH PEAR, PANCETTA AND ROCKET 51

BEETROOT CARPACCIO
with Cured Salmon 52

MUSHROOM RAVIOLI IN PORCINI BROTH 55

SCOTCH EGG
with Herb Mayonnaise 56

PUMPKIN RAVIOLI
with Sage Butter 59

PRAWN CAKES
with Peanut and Lime Dipping Sauce 60

GREEN PAPAYA SALAD
with Salt and Pepper Prawns 63

GRILLED SCAMPI
with Sambal Beans 64

CHICKEN LIVERS
with Port and Prosciutto 67

PRAWNS, AVOCADO AND PINK GRAPEFRUIT 68

ZUCCHINI AND POTATO RÖSTI STACK
with Smoked Salmon and Crème Fraîche 71

MAINS 73

HANDMADE SICILIAN PORK AND FENNEL SAUSAGES with Creamy Leek Mash 74

GRILLED SWORDFISH with Eggplant and Anchovies 77

SALMON FISH FINGERS with Cold Soba Noodles 78

PAN-FRIED BLUE-EYE TREVALLA with Caramelised Fennel 81

BEEF SUKIYAKI 82

PROSCIUTTO, APPLE AND GORGONZOLA PORK CHOPS with Asparagus and Pea Risotto 85

MULLOWAY with Celeriac Purée and Beurre Rouge 86

PROSCIUTTO-WRAPPED CHICKEN with Garlic Mash and Snow Peas 89

CAJUN JAMBALAYA 90

MASSAMAN CURRY with Roti and Pickled Salad 93

JERK CHICKEN with Coconut Rice and Pineapple Salsa 95

CRAB CONGEE 99

PASTA WITH CHORIZO AND PESTO 100

BAHARAT BEEF with Sweet Potato Mash and Mint Yoghurt Sauce 103

NASI GORENG 104

HAINAN CHICKEN with Three Sauces 107

POACHED PORK BELLY with Green Beans and Brandy Sauce 108

LAMB ROULADE with Barley, Smoked Carrots and Mint Pesto 111

HAPUKU WITH BLACK OLIVE SAUCE Veggie Chips and Roasted Tomatoes 114

PAN-SEARED SWORDFISH with Green Curry and Vietnamese Salad 117

JAPANESE-INSPIRED POACHED CHICKEN IN A MUSHROOM BROTH 118

BAKED MOUSSAKA with Greek Salad 121

SPICED KANGAROO with Garam Masala Potatoes and Kachumber Salad 122

PAN-SEARED SALMON with Roasted Beetroot and Freekeh Salad 125

SCAMPI RISOTTO 126

PORK CHEEK with Apple Cider Jus, Crackling and Potato Croquettes 129

LAMB RACK with Green Olive Gremolata and Pommes Dauphine 133

KERALAN FISH MOILEE with Lemon Rice 134

MEXICAN PORK RIBS with White Beans and Pickled Onions 137

PORK FILLET with Orange and Fennel Slaw and Potato Rösti 138

CRISPY BARRAMUNDI with Apple and Mango Salad 141

CHINESE BRAISED BEEF RIBS 142

MORETON BAY BUGS with Celeriac Remoulade and Seafood Bisque 145

TEA-SMOKED DUCK with Fennel Purée and Cranberries 146

SEARED LAMB
with Feta, Beetroot and Rosemary Honey 149

CONFIT SALMON
with Roasted Fennel and Avocado Mousse 150

BEEF CHEEKS
with Port and Celeriac Purée 153

CURED KINGFISH
with Yellow Curry 154

QUAIL
with Corn and Jus 157

RED MULLET
with Jerusalem Artichoke and Basil 158

CONFIT DUCK LEG
with Honey-glazed Beetroot
and Compressed Watermelon 163

DESSERTS 167

TWICE-BAKED GORGONZOLA SOUFFLÉS
with Caramelised Pear and Vermouth 169

CHOCOLATE MOUSSE CAKE
with Poached Pears and Crème Fraîche 170

ZEPPOLE
(Italian Potato Doughnuts) 173

SPICED COFFEE-SOAKED DATES
with Sesame and Cinnamon Cookies 174

SAKE FIGS 177

BLUEBERRY BRIOCHE CUP
with Labneh 178

BANANA TARTLETS
with Mascarpone Cream and Praline 181

MACARONS SIX WAYS 183

CHOCOLATE HAZELNUT CAKE 187

CHOCOLATE RASPBERRY POP DELIGHT 189

YOGHURT PANNACOTTA
with Lemon Zest Jelly, White
Peaches and Thyme Syrup 193

STRAWBERRY AND AMARETTO SEMIFREDDO 194

CHOCOLATE PEPPERMINT DELICE 197

RED VELVET WITH CHOCOLATE AND RASPBERRIES 199

RASPBERRY AND WHITE CHOCOLATE CHEESECAKE
with Chocolate Shards 203

FRIED APPLE PIE
with Salted Caramel 205

DEB'S TRIFLE 209

PETIT APPLE LATTICE PIES
with Spiced Crème Anglaise 210

CHOCOLATE RAVIOLI
with Chocolate Sauce and Orange 213

STRAWBERRY CHAMPAGNE TRIFLE 214

PEACH AND APRICOT TARTE TATIN
with Cinnamon Ice-cream 217

DECONSTRUCTED CHOCOLATE AND RHUBARB TART 219

PEACHES AND CREAM 223

INDEX 226

MKR
MY KITCHEN RULES

APPETISERS, SIDES AND SALADS

Fried eschalots are available at Asian grocers.

TURKEY SAN CHOI BOW

WITH FRIED WONTON SKINS

PREP 30 MINS   COOK 15 MINS   SERVES 4–6

250g jasmine rice, washed
peanut oil, for deep-frying
12 wonton skins, cut into triangular quarters
2 heads baby cos lettuce, leaves separated and washed

TURKEY FILLING

300g turkey mince
2 tbsp dark soy sauce
2 cloves garlic, peeled and finely chopped
1 tbsp peanut oil
1 small brown onion, peeled and finely chopped
2cm piece ginger, peeled and finely chopped
1 carrot, peeled and diced
1 bird's-eye chilli, finely chopped
225g can water chestnuts, drained and chopped
225g can bamboo shoots, drained and chopped
1 tbsp oyster sauce
1 tsp brown sugar
2 tsp sesame oil
1 small red capsicum, deseeded and diced
1 small yellow capsicum, deseeded and diced
1 small zucchini, trimmed and diced
100g punnet enoki mushrooms
100g punnet shiitake mushrooms, sliced
2 tsp cornflour
250g bean shoots

bean shoots and fried eschalots, to garnish

1 Cook the rice according to the directions on the packet. Drain and set aside.

2 Heat the peanut oil in a frying pan or wok and deep-fry the wonton skins until crisp and golden. Drain on paper towel.

3 To prepare the turkey filling, combine the turkey mince, dark soy and half the garlic in a small bowl. Refrigerate, covered, for 30 minutes.

4 Heat the peanut oil in a large saucepan over medium heat. Cook the onion, ginger, carrot, chilli and remaining garlic, stirring, until fragrant and soft. Add the turkey and cook until browned.

5 Stir in the water chestnuts, bamboo shoots, oyster sauce, sugar and sesame oil then add the remaining vegetables. Cook, stirring occasionally, for 5 minutes, or until the vegetables are tender. Add the cornflour combined with 2 teaspoons of water and stir-fry for 1 minute, or until thickened. Stir in the bean shoots.

6 To assemble, place a thin layer of rice on each lettuce leaf and top with the turkey filling. Garnish with bean shoots, fried eschalots and fried wonton skins and serve.

PHỞ ON THE GO

PREP 30 MINS COOK 1 HOUR SERVES 4–6

1 bunch spring onions, white part only, trimmed and coarsely chopped
2 tsp rice flour
salt and pepper, to taste
vegetable oil, for shallow-frying
160g bean shoots
250g beef fillet, thinly sliced

BROTH
750ml water
500g gravy beef or chuck steak, thinly sliced
2 tbsp fish sauce
1½ tbsp light soy sauce
3 star anise
2cm piece galangal, peeled and chopped
10 peppercorns
½ bunch coriander roots, trimmed and chopped

NOODLES
1 cup rice flour
1 tbsp cornflour
½ tsp salt
310ml cold water
1 tbsp light olive oil

CHILLI SAUCE
4 long red chillies, trimmed
2 cloves garlic, peeled
2 tsp rice vinegar
2 tsp caster sugar

coriander and mint leaves, to serve
lime wedges, to serve

1 To make the broth, bring all the ingredients to the boil in a large saucepan. Simmer, covered, for 1 hour. Strain and discard the solids. Season with extra soy or fish sauce if desired.

2 Meanwhile, to make noodles, sift together the flours and salt in a large bowl. Slowly whisk in the water and oil until the mixture is smooth and silky.

3 Pour ¼ cup of the mixture into a cold, non-stick frying pan. Cook, covered, over medium heat, until the mixture bubbles. Flip the pancake onto a tray lined with baking paper. Repeat with the remaining batter, cooling the pan under cold water between batches. Cut the rice pancakes into thin strips to form noodles.

4 To make the chilli sauce, cook all the ingredients in a small saucepan over low heat until the garlic is soft. Season to taste. Crush using a mortar and pestle until smooth.

5 To make crispy spring onions, combine the spring onion and rice flour in a small bowl and season to taste. Shallow-fry ¼ teaspoonfuls of the mixture until golden and crisp. Drain on paper towel.

6 To serve, divide the bean shoots among serving dishes. Top with the noodles and raw beef then pour over the boiling broth. Garnish with coriander, mint and crispy spring onions. Serve with chilli sauce and lime wedges.

SEASON 2 · ESTHER & ALI

The tomato relish can be made up to a week in advance. Store, covered, in the refrigerator. Serve any leftover relish with burgers, sausages or steak.

CORN, ZUCCHINI AND HALOUMI FRITTERS

WITH SMOKY TOMATO RELISH AND AVOCADO CREAM

PREP 45 MINS COOK 1 HOUR 20 MINS SERVES 4–6

RELISH

500g roma tomatoes, halved
2 tbsp olive oil
salt and pepper, to taste
1 small onion, peeled and sliced
1 small red capsicum, deseeded and diced
2 tsp brown mustard seeds
100ml red wine vinegar
80g brown sugar
2 tsp sweet paprika
½ tsp allspice
juice of ¼ lemon

FRITTERS

50ml milk
1 egg
1 corn cob, kernels stripped
1 small zucchini, trimmed and grated
90g haloumi, cut into 1cm cubes
1 spring onion, trimmed and sliced
60g ricotta cheese, crumbled
120g can creamed corn
2 tbsp chopped chives
2 tbsp chopped parsley
½ tsp ground cumin
¼ tsp sweet paprika
50g self-raising flour
olive oil, for frying

PROSCIUTTO-WRAPPED ASPARAGUS

1 bunch large asparagus, trimmed and sliced lengthways
5 slices prosciutto, halved lengthways
1 tbsp olive oil

AVOCADO CREAM

1 avocado
1 tbsp crème fraîche
¼ tsp chilli sauce
juice of ½ lime

rocket leaves, to serve
juice of ½ lemon, to serve

1. To make the relish, preheat the oven to 220°C. Line a baking tray with baking paper.
2. Place the tomatoes, cut side up, on the prepared tray. Drizzle with 1 tablespoon oil and season to taste. Roast for 30 minutes, or until golden and soft. Cool slightly then remove the skins and chop coarsely.
3. Heat the remaining oil in a large saucepan over medium heat. Cook the onion for 5–10 minutes, or until golden brown. Add the capsicum and cook for a further 5 minutes, or until soft. Add the mustard seeds and roasted tomatoes. Cook, stirring occasionally, for 5 minutes. Add the remaining ingredients and bring to the boil. Reduce the heat and simmer, uncovered, for 30 minutes, or until thickened. Cool completely.
4. Meanwhile, to make the fritters, whisk together the milk and egg in a bowl.

continued next page ➤

CORN, ZUCCHINI AND HALOUMI FRITTERS
WITH SMOKY TOMATO RELISH AND AVOCADO CREAM
(continued)

5 In a separate bowl, combine the corn kernels, zucchini, haloumi, spring onion, ricotta, creamed corn, herbs and spices. Stir in the flour. Add the egg mixture. Stir thoroughly to combine and season to taste.

6 Heat a lightly oiled frying pan over medium–high heat. Spoon a tablespoon of the fritter mixture into the pan and cook until the underside is golden. Turn and cook for 2–3 minutes, or until cooked through. Remove from the pan and repeat with the remaining batter.

7 Preheat the oven to 180°C. To make the prosciutto-wrapped asparagus, wrap each halved asparagus spear with half a slice of prosciutto. Place the wrapped asparagus in an ovenproof tray, drizzle with oil and season to taste. Cook in the oven for 10 minutes, or until the prosciutto is crisp and asparagus is golden.

8 To make the avocado cream, process all the ingredients in a food processor until smooth. Season to taste.

9 Arrange the fritters on serving plates. Top with relish and avocado cream and serve with the wrapped asparagus and rocket leaves dressed with lemon juice.

GRANDMA'S BRANDY PÂTÉ
WITH HOMEMADE BRIOCHE AND CHUTNEY

PREP 40 MINS COOK 40 MINS + 3 HOURS CHILLING + 2 HOURS 30 MINS PROVING SERVES 8

170g butter
2 onions, peeled and finely chopped
460g chicken livers, cleaned
6 bacon rashers, finely chopped
120g mushrooms, finely chopped
½ tsp thyme leaves
2 bay leaves
2 tbsp port
2 tbsp dry sherry
2 tbsp brandy
250ml pure cream
salt and pepper, to taste

BLACKBERRY CHUTNEY

500g blackberries
2 large apples, peeled, cored and finely chopped
140g caster sugar
1 medium red onion, peeled and finely chopped
1cm piece fresh ginger, peeled and grated
2 tbsp Dijon mustard
150ml white wine vinegar

BRIOCHE ROLLS

60ml warm milk
10g dried yeast
2 tsp caster sugar
300g bread flour
1 tsp salt
3 eggs, plus 1 extra, lightly beaten
500g butter, softened and cut into 1cm cubes

thyme leaves or micro herbs, to serve

1 To make the pâté, melt the butter in a large frying pan over medium heat. Add the onion and cook, stirring, for 5 minutes, or until softened. Add the chicken livers, bacon, mushrooms, thyme and bay leaves. Cook, stirring occasionally, for 2 minutes, or until the livers are browned all over. Remove the bay leaves and transfer the mixture to a food processor.

2 Add the port, sherry and brandy to the pan and simmer for 30 seconds, or until reduced by half. Add to the food processor with the cream and process until smooth. Season with salt and pepper. Strain through a sieve into a jug, then divide among 8 ramekins. Refrigerate for 3 hours or overnight until set.

3 To make the chutney, combine all the ingredients except the vinegar in a large saucepan. Stir over medium heat for 4 minutes, or until softened and the blackberries burst. Stir in the vinegar and season with salt and pepper. Simmer, uncovered, for 10 minutes, or until slightly reduced. Set aside to cool.

4 To make the brioche rolls, combine the milk, yeast and sugar in a small bowl. Set aside for 5 minutes or until frothy.

5 Sift the flour and salt into the bowl of an electric mixer. Add the yeast mixture and 3 eggs. Using the paddle attachment, mix on low speed for 3 minutes. With the motor running, add the butter, 1 cube at a time, until the dough is smooth and shiny.

6 Knead the dough on a lightly floured surface for 30 seconds. Place the dough in a greased bowl and cover with cling film. Set aside in a warm, draught-free place for 2 hours, or until dough doubles in size.

7 Preheat the oven to 200°C. Punch down the dough, turn out onto a lightly floured work surface and knead for 10 minutes, or until the dough is smooth and elastic. Divide into 8 portions. Using floured hands, roll each portion into 3 balls.

continued next page ➤

GRANDMA'S BRANDY PÂTÉ

WITH HOMEMADE BRIOCHE AND CHUTNEY

(continued)

8 Place 3 balls side by side into one hole of a greased 80ml (⅓ cup) capacity muffin pan. Repeat with the remaining dough. Cover the pan with a clean tea towel and set aside for 20 minutes, or until risen by half.

9 Brush the brioche with beaten egg and bake for 15 minutes, or until golden.

10 Garnish the pâté with thyme leaves or micro herbs and serve with chutney and brioche on the side.

The chutney recipe makes 5 cups, so you can use the extra leftover chutney to make a great gift. Pour hot chutney into sterilised jars and seal immediately. Refrigerate for up to two weeks.

MUSHROOM SOUP
WITH GOAT'S CHEESE CROUTONS

PREP 10 MINS COOK 35 MINS SERVES 4

100g pearl barley
10g dried porcini mushrooms
1 tbsp olive oil
500g eye fillet steak, cut into 1cm cubes
1 large onion, peeled and finely chopped
3 cloves garlic, peeled and finely chopped
200g field mushrooms, trimmed and sliced
150g Swiss brown mushrooms, trimmed and sliced
500ml beef stock
250ml water
2 tbsp finely chopped tarragon
2 tbsp finely chopped thyme
2 tbsp finely chopped parsley
1 tbsp lemon juice
salt and pepper, to taste

GOAT'S CHEESE CROUTONS

40g butter
2 onions, peeled and thinly sliced
1 tbsp brown sugar
4 slices baguette-style crusty bread
50g goat's cheese
1 tbsp finely chopped thyme

finely chopped tarragon, thyme and parsley, to serve

1 Place the pearl barley and porcini in separate bowls of water, to soak, until required.

2 Heat a large, lightly oiled saucepan until very hot. Cook the beef in three batches, stirring each batch for 30 seconds, or until just browned. Remove and set aside.

3 Reduce the heat and add the remaining olive oil to the same saucepan. Cook the onion and garlic, stirring, until the onion is soft. Add the mushrooms. Cook, stirring, for 5 minutes, or until soft and golden.

4 Drain the barley and add to the pan.

5 Drain the porcini mushrooms, reserving the liquid. Slice the mushrooms thinly then add to the pan with the reserved liquid, along with the stock, water and herbs.

6 Simmer, covered, for 30 minutes, or until the barley is tender and the soup has thickened slightly. Stir in the cooked beef and lemon juice. Season to taste.

7 Meanwhile, to make the croutons, melt the butter in a medium saucepan. Cook the onions over medium heat for 2–3 minutes, or until soft. Add the sugar and cook, stirring occasionally, for 10 minutes, or until golden brown and caramelised. Season to taste.

8 Combine the goat's cheese and thyme in a bowl. Grill the bread slices on one side under a hot grill until golden brown. Turn over and spread with the goat's cheese and thyme. Top with a little caramelised onion. Cook under a hot grill until golden. Stir any remaining caramelised onion into the soup.

9 Scatter extra fresh herbs over the soup and serve with the goat's cheese croutons.

The eye fillet steaks can be substituted with diced lamb fillet. Soak barley in water overnight to speed up the cooking process.
SEASON 2 · ASH & KELLY

To cook the damper the traditional way, shape the four portions of dough into sausage shapes and coil them around the end of a stick, pressing the coil together so there are no gaps. Wrap with greased foil. Hold the damper over the coals, turning, for about 15 minutes or until it is golden brown and crisp when checked.

BREAKFAST DAMPER
WITH TOMATO RELISH

PREP 10 MINS COOK 20 MINS SERVES 4

- 2 tsp olive oil
- 200g thick bacon, diced into small cubes
- 1 eschalot, peeled and finely chopped
- 1 clove garlic, peeled and crushed
- 1 tbsp chopped rosemary
- 300g self-raising flour
- salt and pepper, to taste
- 125ml beer
- 125ml lemonade
- 4 fried eggs

TOMATO RELISH

- 1 tbsp olive oil
- 2 eschalots, peeled and finely chopped
- 1 clove garlic, peeled and finely chopped
- 1 small red chilli, trimmed and chopped
- 1 tbsp finely chopped fresh rosemary
- 1 tbsp finely chopped fresh thyme
- 1 tbsp finely chopped fresh basil
- 1 tsp dried bush tomato
- 400g can chopped tomatoes
- 100g tomato passata
- 1 tsp white wine vinegar

1. Preheat the oven to 220°C. To make the damper, heat the oil in a medium frying pan over medium heat. Cook the bacon, eschalot and garlic until the bacon is brown and crisp. Stir in the rosemary.
2. Season the flour in a large bowl. Slowly add the beer and lemonade and mix until just combined. Turn the dough out onto a lightly floured work surface. Sprinkle over the bacon mixture. Knead lightly until smooth and combined.
3. Divide the dough into 4 portions. Roll each portion into ball or oval shapes. Cook on a baking tray lined with baking paper for about 15 minutes, or until golden and crisp and a skewer comes out clean once inserted.
4. To make the relish, heat the oil in a medium frying pan over medium heat. Cook the eschalots, garlic and chilli for 2–3 minutes, or until soft. Add the herbs, canned tomatoes, passata and vinegar. Simmer for approximately 10 minutes, or until thickened.
5. Serve the damper with tomato relish and fried eggs.

SALT AND PEPPER MUD CRAB
WITH CHILLI SOY DIPPING SAUCE

PREP 50 MINS COOK 10 MINS SERVES 4

1 tbsp sea salt
1 tbsp ground black pepper
1 tbsp white pepper
2 mud crabs
¼ cup cornflour
vegetable oil, for deep-frying
1 brown onion, peeled and finely chopped
3 spring onions, trimmed and thinly sliced
1 long red chilli, finely chopped
5cm piece ginger, peeled and grated
5 cloves garlic, peeled and crushed

CHILLI SOY DIPPING SAUCE

120ml light soy sauce
2 tbsp mirin
2 tbsp oyster sauce
2 tbsp caster sugar
2 tsp sesame oil
½ long red chilli, chopped

1. To make the dipping sauce, combine the ingredients in a small bowl. Set aside.
2. Combine half the salt and peppers in another small bowl and set aside.
3. To prepare the crabs, use a cleaver to cut away the claws. Crack the claws lightly (this will allow the flavours to penetrate).
4. Remove the top shell from body by releasing the flap on underside. Remove and discard the grey gills. Rinse the crab lightly then cut the body in half. Lightly dry all the crab pieces with paper towel. Place in a large bowl and toss with cornflour.
5. Deep-fry the crab pieces in batches until they just change colour. Drain on paper towel.
6. Heat the oil in a wok over high heat. Stir-fry the onions, chilli, ginger and garlic for 1 minute. Add the remaining salt and peppers and stir-fry for 30 seconds. Add the crab pieces and toss to coat.
7. Serve the crab with the dipping sauce and the salt and peppers mixture.

Mud crabs are found from the north of Australia right round to Sydney. The peak season for the Northern Territory is May to August and Queensland and New South Wales is January to April.

If you can't find jinhua ham at your local Asian grocer, substitute prosciutto. Salt-cured fish is available at Asian grocers and in the Asian food section of some major supermarkets.

STEAMED OYSTERS

WITH VERMICELLI AND XO SAUCE, MUSHROOMS AND CHINESE GREENS

PREP 1 HOUR + SOAKING TIME   COOK 45 MINS   SERVES 4

4 large oysters, on the half shell

XO SAUCE

125g dried scallops, soaked overnight in 375ml Shaoxing wine
50g dried shrimp, soaked in water overnight
60ml peanut oil
1 small red onion, peeled and finely chopped
75g cloves garlic, peeled and finely chopped
2 red bird's-eye chillies, finely chopped
3 tsp chilli flakes
25g piece jinhua ham, finely chopped
25g salt-cured fish, finely chopped
½ tsp ground Sichuan pepper
125ml water
1½ tbsp caster sugar

VERMICELLI NOODLES

250ml chicken stock
75g dried vermicelli noodles
1 tsp vegetable oil

MUSHROOMS AND CHINESE GREENS

1 tbsp peanut oil
2 cloves garlic, finely chopped
1cm piece fresh ginger, peeled and finely chopped
2 baby bok choy, ends trimmed and halved lengthways
4 dried shiitake mushrooms, soaked in water overnight and drained
½ cup oyster sauce
1 tbsp sugar
1 tbsp Shaoxing wine

sliced spring onion, fried eschalots and coriander, to garnish

1 To make XO sauce, drain the scallops and reserve the liquid. Shred the scallops by hand. Drain the shrimp and finely chop (discarding the liquid).

2 Heat the oil in a wok over medium heat. Stir-fry the onion, garlic and shrimps for 3–5 minutes, or until the mixture stops steaming. Add the chillies, chilli flakes, ham and fish and cook over low heat for 10 minutes, or until the mixture is very soft. Stir in the scallops and pepper then add the water, sugar and 3 tablespoons of the reserved scallop liquid. Simmer, watching continuously to prevent burning, until the mixture has reduced to a thick chunky sauce. Adjust seasoning with chilli, sugar or soy if required (the flavours should be a balance of spicy, sweet and salty).

3 Gently rinse the oysters. Cook, covered, in a baking paper-lined bamboo steamer, over a saucepan of simmering water for 5 minutes, or until just cooked.

4 Bring the stock to the boil in a medium-sized saucepan. Add the noodles and cook until tender. Drain and reserve the stock. Heat the oil in a wok over medium heat. Add 1 tablespoon of the XO sauce and cook for 30 seconds. Add the noodles and stir-fry to coat in the sauce.

5 To cook the mushrooms and greens, clean the wok and heat half the oil over medium heat. Stir-fry the garlic and ginger until fragrant. Add the bok choy and stir-fry until just wilted. Remove from the wok. Add the mushrooms and stir-fry for 1 minute. Add the oyster sauce, sugar and 2 tablespoons of the reserved chicken stock and simmer until the liquid has reduced by half. Stir in the Shaoxing wine.

6 To serve, top the oysters with noodles and XO sauce. Garnish with spring onions, fried eschalots and coriander and serve with the mushrooms and greens.

AGEDASHI TOFU
WITH PORK GYOZA

PREP 1 HOUR COOK 15 MINS SERVES 4–6

300g silken tofu
1 cup panko breadcrumbs
1 tbsp cornflour
salt and pepper, to taste
vegetable oil, for deep-frying

GYOZA

200g pork mince
100g water chestnuts, drained and finely chopped
½ cup finely chopped wombok (Chinese cabbage)
5 fresh shiitake mushrooms, finely chopped
½ small brown onion, peeled and finely chopped
¼ cup finely chopped coriander
1 clove garlic, peeled and crushed
½ cm piece fresh ginger, peeled and grated
2 tbsp oyster sauce
2 tsp sesame oil
1 tsp cornflour
18 round dumpling wrappers
peanut oil, for frying

AGEDASHI SAUCE

500ml water
15g kombu
2 tbsp bonito flakes
60ml soy sauce
60ml mirin

bonito flakes, sliced spring onions, fresh seaweed salad and pickled daikon, to garnish

1 To make the *gyoza*, combine all ingredients except the wrappers and peanut oil in a medium-sized bowl. Place a heaped teaspoon of the mixture into the centre of each wrapper. Brush the edges with water, then fold in half and pinch the edges to seal.

2 Gently wrap the tofu in paper towel to drain excess water. You may need to repeat this to remove all the water.

3 To make the *agedashi* sauce, first make a dashi broth by bringing the water and kombu to the boil in a small saucepan. As soon as water boils, remove the kombu. Add the bonito flakes and remove from the heat. As soon as the flakes have sunk to bottom of pan, strain.

4 Place 125ml of the dashi broth in a saucepan with the soy sauce and mirin. Bring to the boil then remove from the heat.

5 Heat a thin layer of peanut oil in a non-stick frying pan. Cook the *gyoza* in a single layer until golden brown on both sides and cooked through, turning only once so you achieve a golden crust. Add 2 tablespoons of water to the pan. Cook, covered, for 1 minute, or until the *gyoza* are cooked through.

6 Cut the tofu into 3cm x 4cm pieces. Combine the breadcrumbs and cornflour in a bowl and season to taste. Coat the tofu in the breadcrumb mixture. Heat the oil in a medium fry pan and deep-fry until golden brown. Drain on paper towel.

7 Drizzle the tofu with the *agedashi* sauce and serve with the *gyoza*. Garnish with bonito flakes and spring onions and decorate the plate with pickled sliced daikon and fresh seaweed salad.

The gyoza can be made a day in advance. Store in single layers, separated by baking paper, in an airtight container in the refrigerator. Alternatively, freeze for up to two months.

Serve with a green salad to turn this dish into a light main course.

SAGANAKI PRAWNS
WITH TOMATO, FETA AND HOMEMADE CRUSTY BREAD

PREP 40 MINS + PROVING TIME COOK 35 MINS SERVES 4

80ml extra-virgin olive oil
12 green banana prawns, peeled and deveined, tails intact
6 large garlic cloves, peeled and crushed
1 tbsp tomato paste
2 bay leaves
1 punnet large cherry tomatoes, quartered
cracked black pepper, to taste
80g feta, crumbled

BREAD

1½ tsp sugar
7g sachet dried yeast
310ml warm water
1 tbsp olive oil
450g plain flour
1 tsp salt
cornmeal, for dusting

parsley or micro herbs, to garnish

1 To make the bread, combine the sugar, yeast and 125ml of the water in a small bowl. Stand for 5–10 minutes, or until frothy. Transfer to a large bowl and stir in the oil and remaining water. Add the flour and salt, stir to combine, then use your hands to bring dough together.

2 Turn the dough out onto a lightly floured work surface and knead for 10 minutes, or until the dough is smooth and elastic. Place the dough in a greased bowl and cover with plastic wrap. Set aside in a warm, draught-free place for 1½ hours, or until the dough doubles in size. Punch down to release air, then turn out onto a lightly floured work surface and knead lightly.

3 Divide the dough in half, then shape each half into a 15cm-long loaf. Dust work surface with cornmeal and sit the base of each loaf on top (the cornmeal will give it a crunchy base). Place each loaf on a greased oven tray, cover with a tea towel and stand for 35 minutes.

4 Meanwhile, preheat the oven to 180°C. Bake the loaves for 35 minutes, or until golden brown and sound hollow when tapped on the base.

5 To make the prawns, heat 1½ tablespoons of the oil in a large, deep pan over medium–high heat. Add the prawns and cook, turning once, for 1–2 minutes, or until just changed in colour but not cooked through. Remove the prawns from pan, then allow pan to cool for 2 minutes.

6 Return the pan to low heat and add the garlic and remaining oil. Cook gently for 5 minutes, then add the tomato paste and bay leaves. Increase the heat to medium and cook, stirring, for a further 3 minutes.

7 Increase heat to medium–high and add the tomatoes. Cook for 5 minutes, or until tomatoes begin to break down. Remove the bay leaves and season with pepper. Stir in the prawns and cook for 1 minute, or until cooked through. Stir in the feta and remove from the heat.

8 Scatter the prawns, tomato and feta with fresh parsley or micro herbs and serve with the warm crusty bread on the side.

WARM DUCK SALAD
WITH BEETROOT, POMEGRANATE AND REDCURRANT VINAIGRETTE

PREP 30 MINS COOK 40 MINS SERVES 4

125ml balsamic vinegar
30g caster sugar
¼ tsp ground nutmeg
250ml water
8 baby beetroot, trimmed
200g green beans
4 duck breast fillets
2 tsp Chinese five-spice powder
100g baby salad leaves
120g Danish feta, cut into 1cm cubes
3 tbsp chopped walnuts, roasted

VINAIGRETTE

2 tbsp extra-virgin olive oil
2 tbsp pomegranate juice
2 tbsp redcurrant jelly, warmed, sieved
1 tbsp sherry vinegar
1 tsp Dijon mustard
salt and pepper, to taste

pomegranate seeds, to serve

1. Place the vinegar, sugar, nutmeg and water in a medium-sized saucepan over low heat and stir until the sugar dissolves. Add the beetroot and place a round of baking paper on top. Simmer for 25 minutes, or until tender. Drain, then cool. Peel the beetroot and cut into quarters.
2. Meanwhile, cook the green beans in a saucepan of salted boiling water for 3–4 minutes, or until tender. Drain, then transfer to a bowl of iced water for 5 minutes. Drain.
3. To make the vinaigrette, whisk all the ingredients in a small bowl until combined. Season with salt and pepper.
4. Using a sharp knife, lightly score the duck skin, then season with salt and five-spice powder.
5. Place the duck, skin-side down, in a non-stick frying pan over low–medium heat. Cook for 8 minutes, or until the fat has melted and the skin is crisp. Turn and cook for a further 4–5 minutes, then transfer to a warm plate. Rest, covered, for 5 minutes, then slice.
6. Arrange the beans, beetroot, salad leaves, feta and walnuts on a serving plate. Top with duck and drizzle with vinaigrette. Scatter with pomegranate seeds to serve.

To extract juice from a pomegranate, lightly squeeze over a regular citrus juicer – one pomegranate will yield about 125ml juice. To extract seeds from a pomegranate, place chunks in a bowl of cold water. Using your hands, separate seeds from the membrane (the membrane will float to the top for easy removal).

SEASON 3 · ANGELA & JUSTINE

You can cook the noodles and toss with the dressing up to 1 day in advance. Store, covered, in the refrigerator. This will give the noodles a chance to absorb some of the great flavours, then stir in capsicum and herbs before serving.

CRISPY CHICKEN
ON ASIAN RICE NOODLE SALAD

PREP 25 MINS COOK 10 MINS SERVES 4

100g vermicelli noodles
1 red capsicum, deseeded and thinly sliced
2 tbsp chopped chives
½ cup coriander leaves
½ cup mint leaves
½ cup Thai basil leaves

DRESSING

2 tbsp lime juice
2 tbsp fish sauce
1 tbsp caster sugar
1cm piece fresh ginger, peeled and finely grated
½ long red chilli, finely chopped

CRISPY CHICKEN

1 egg
1cm piece fresh ginger, peeled and finely grated
1 clove garlic, peeled and crushed
¾ cup plain flour
2 tsp Chinese five-spice powder
2 tsp sea salt flakes
1 tsp freshly ground black pepper
2 large chicken breasts, thinly sliced
vegetable oil, for shallow-frying

1. To make the dressing, whisk all the ingredients in a small bowl until the sugar dissolves.
2. Place the noodles in a large bowl, cover with boiling water and stand for 5 minutes. Drain, then return to the bowl. Add the dressing and toss to combine. Add the capsicum and herbs and toss to combine.
3. To make the crispy chicken, whisk the egg, ginger and garlic in a large bowl until just combined. Combine the flour, five-spice powder, salt and pepper in a separate large bowl. Dip the chicken pieces in the egg mixture, drain off excess, then toss in the flour mixture.
4. Fill a wok or deep frying pan halfway with oil and shallow-fry the chicken, in batches, for 2–3 minutes, or until golden and cooked through. Drain on paper towel.
5. Divide the noodle salad among four serving bowls and top with the chicken.

SEARED MOROCCAN TUNA
AND CURED SALMON

PREP 1 HOUR COOK 25 MINS SERVES 4

200g piece sashimi-grade tuna, about 3cm thick
2 tsp olive oil
200g piece sashimi-grade salmon, about 3cm thick, pin-boned
juice of ½ lime

MAYONNAISE

2 egg yolks
½ tsp Dijon mustard
1 tsp white wine vinegar
200ml vegetable oil
salt and pepper, to taste
1 tsp ground cumin
2 tsp lemon juice
2 tsp avocado oil

SALAD FOR SALMON

2 tsp olive oil
½ zucchini, trimmed and cut into 1cm cubes
½ red capsicum, deseeded and cut into 1cm pieces
1 small eschalot, peeled and cut into 1cm pieces
juice of ½ lemon
2 tbsp coarsely chopped coriander leaves
½ long red chilli, finely chopped
½ long green chilli, finely chopped

SALAD FOR TUNA

½ tsp ground cumin
1 tbsp olive oil
½ small eggplant, trimmed and cut into 1cm dice
1 truss tomato, peeled, deseeded and chopped
2 tbsp coarsely chopped flat-leaf parsley
juice of ½ lemon

salmon roe, to garnish

1. To make the mayonnaise, combine the egg yolks, mustard and vinegar in a food processor. With the motor running, slowly drizzle in the vegetable oil, processing until the mixture is thick and combined. Season with salt and pepper.
2. Divide the mayonnaise between two bowls. Stir the cumin and half the lemon juice into one bowl of mayonnaise. Stir the avocado oil and remaining lemon juice into the other bowl.
3. To prepare the salad for the salmon, heat the olive oil in a frying pan over medium–high heat. Cook the vegetables, stirring occasionally, for 2–3 minutes, or until just tender. Remove from the heat and transfer to a bowl. Stir in the remaining ingredients. Season to taste and set aside.
4. To prepare the salad for the tuna, dry-fry the cumin in a small frying pan over medium heat for 1 minute until fragrant. Set aside. Heat 2 teaspoons of the olive oil in a frying pan over medium–high heat. Cook the eggplant, stirring occasionally, until golden brown. Remove and place in a bowl.
5. Add the remaining oil to the same frying pan over high heat. Add the tomato, parsley and cumin. Cook for 1 minute. Add the mixture to the eggplant. Stir in the lemon juice and season to taste.
6. Cut the tuna into 3cm-square diameter logs and season to taste. Heat a lightly oiled non-stick frying pan over high heat. Cook the tuna logs for about 10 seconds on all sides until seared. Remove from the heat. Stand for 5 minutes, then cut into 5mm slices.
7. Cut the salmon into 5mm slices. Toss with the lime juice and season to taste. Divide the salads and fish among 4 plates. Serve the avocado mayonnaise with the salmon and the cumin mayonnaise with the tuna. Garnish with salmon roe and serve.

If you prefer a milder dish, remove the seeds and membranes from the chillies.

To segment the grapefruit, cut off the ends so the fruit sits flat. Using a sharp knife, cut away the white pith and skin. Hold the fruit over a bowl and cut down either side of white membrane to remove the segments. Squeeze the remaining fruit to extract juice.

ZESTY PRAWN SALAD

PREP 1 HOUR   COOK 2 MINS   SERVES 4

CHILLI LIME AIOLI

3 egg yolks
2 tbsp lime juice
2 tsp Dijon mustard
1 large clove garlic, peeled and crushed
a pinch of chilli flakes
250ml olive oil
salt and pepper, to taste

DRESSING

60ml lime juice
2 tbsp finely grated palm sugar
3 tsp soy sauce
2 tsp fish sauce
½ tsp finely grated fresh ginger
1 Thai red chilli, finely chopped

ZESTY PRAWNS

12 large green prawns, shelled and deveined
1 tbsp olive oil
1 tsp finely grated lime zest
1 tsp lime juice

SALAD

2 small ripe avocados, peeled, deseeded and cut into 2cm dice
2 ruby grapefruit, peeled and segmented
1 Thai red chilli, seeds removed and thinly sliced

60g baby rocket leaves, to serve
crushed, toasted peanuts, to serve
lemon cheeks, to serve

1. To make the aioli, whisk the yolks, lime juice, mustard, garlic and chilli until combined. Slowly drizzle in the olive oil, whisking continuously until thick and creamy. Season to taste. Refrigerate until required.
2. To make the dressing, whisk the lime juice, palm sugar and sauces in a small bowl until the sugar dissolves. Stir in the ginger and chilli.
3. To prepare the zesty prawns, combine all ingredients in a bowl and season to taste. Heat a large frying pan over high heat. Cook the prawns for 30 seconds on each side, or until just cooked through.
4. To make the salad, place all the ingredients in a bowl. Add 1 tablespoon of the dressing and toss gently to combine.
5. To serve, place a mound of rocket on each serving plate. Top with the prawns, drizzle with a little dressing and sprinkle with nuts. Serve with the avocado and grapefruit salad, aioli and lemon wedges.

VIETNAMESE PORK AND PRAWN PANCAKES

PREP 30 MINUTES + SOAKING TIME SERVES 4–6

⅓ cup dried, split yellow mung beans
800g rindless pork belly
200g small green prawns, shells intact
salt and pepper, to taste
vegetable oil, for frying
250g bean sprouts
4 spring onions, trimmed and finely chopped

DIPPING SAUCE

50g raw sugar
375ml warm water
¼ cup fish sauce
juice of 1 lemon
2 Thai red chillies, deseeded and finely chopped
2 cloves garlic, peeled and finely chopped

PANCAKE BATTER

560ml water
560ml coconut milk
340g rice flour
2 tbsp cornflour
1 tsp ground turmeric
1 tsp sugar
½ tsp salt

butter lettuce leaves, to serve
mint leaves, to serve
coriander leaves, to serve

1 Soak the mung beans in water for 3 hours or overnight. Steam in a sieve over a saucepan of boiling water until tender.

2 To make the dipping sauce, stir the sugar and water in a jug until the sugar dissolves. Stir in the remaining ingredients and set aside.

3 Place the pork belly in a large saucepan of salted boiling water and simmer gently for 25 minutes, or until cooked through. Drain, set aside to cool, then slice thinly.

4 Deep-fry the prawns for 3–5 minutes, or until golden and crisp. Drain on paper towel and season with salt and pepper.

5 To make the pancake batter, whisk all the ingredients in a large bowl until smooth and combined.

6 Heat 2 teaspoons of the vegetable oil in a large non-stick frying pan over medium heat. Add ⅔ cup of the batter and swirl the pan to spread evenly. When the pancake has started to cook and is crisp around the edges, layer the bean sprouts, spring onions, pork, prawns and mung beans on one side. Fold over and slide out of pan onto a serving plate. Repeat with the remaining batter and filling ingredients.

7 Serve the pancakes with lettuce, mint and coriander leaves and dipping sauce.

For a truly authentic taste, try adding some fresh chopped chilli to the salsa with the onion and garlic.

BACON HUEVOS RANCHEROS
WITH BLOODY MARY SALSA

PREP 1 HOUR + RESTING COOK 1 HOUR + RESTING SERVES 4

4 eggs
8 rashers smoked bacon
4 tbsp goat's curd
2 small avocados, peeled, deseeded and cut into wedges

TORTILLAS

250g plain flour
100ml water
1 tbsp olive oil
a pinch salt

SAUCE

1 tbsp lemon juice
1 tbsp lime juice
1 tbsp Worcestershire sauce
1 tsp Tabasco sauce

SALSA

1 tbsp olive oil
100g piece speck, cut into 1cm dice
1 onion, peeled and finely chopped
2 cloves garlic, peeled and crushed
1 red capsicum, deseeded and finely diced
¼ tsp dried mixed spices such as paprika, thyme and oregano
4 medium tomatoes, deseeded and finely diced
1 tsp finely grated lemon zest

½ cup chopped parsley, to garnish
lime wedges, to serve

1 To make the tortillas, mix or process all the ingredients to form a smooth dough. Knead for 5 minutes. Cover with a tea towel and rest for 10 minutes. Divide the dough into four portions and roll each portion into thin rounds.

2 To make the sauce, combine all ingredients in a small jug.

3 To make the salsa, heat the oil in a frying pan over medium heat. Cook the speck for 5 minutes, or until golden brown. Set aside. Add the onion, garlic, capsicum and spices to the same pan. Cook for a approximately 2–3 minutes, or until soft. Stir in the tomatoes and speck and cook, stirring frequently, for 20 minutes, or until the mixture is soft. Remove from the heat and stir in zest and half the sauce.

4 Meanwhile, preheat the oven to 180°C.

5 Heat a large lightly oiled frying pan over medium–high heat. Cook the tortillas, one at a time, on both sides, until golden and crisp.

6 Arrange the tortillas on a large oven tray or individual non-stick pans. Divide the salsa over each tortilla, making a well in centre of the salsa. Crack an egg into each well. Bake for 6–8 minutes, or until the egg is set and cooked to your liking

7 Cook the bacon in a lightly oiled frying pan until browned and crisp.

8 To serve, arrange goat's curd, avocado and bacon onto the egg and salsa. Sprinkle with parsley and serve with lime wedges and the remaining sauce.

VIETNAMESE BAGUETTES

PREP 40 MINUTES COOK 10 MINUTES SERVES 4

4 baby cos lettuce leaves
1 Lebanese cucumber, thinly sliced
4 x 15–20cm baguettes
2 tbsp hoisin sauce

PICKLED VEGETABLES

5 tbsp white vinegar
5 tbsp caster sugar
2 carrots, peeled and julienned
3 red radishes, trimmed and julienned
1 clove garlic, peeled and crushed
1 bird's-eye chilli, finely chopped

MAYONNAISE

2 egg yolks
juice of ½ lemon
1 tsp white vinegar
¼ tsp cayenne pepper
300ml vegetable oil
100ml extra-virgin olive oil
salt and pepper, to taste

PORK PATTIES

250g pork mince
2 bird's-eye chillies, finely chopped
1 stick lemongrass, bruised and finely chopped
2cm piece fresh ginger, peeled and grated
4 cloves garlic, peeled and crushed
2 tsp kecap manis
2 tsp oyster sauce
1 tsp light soy sauce

coriander leaves, to serve

1 To make the pickled vegetables, stir the vinegar and sugar in a large bowl until the sugar dissolves. Stir in the remaining ingredients, then refrigerate until required.

2 To make the mayonnaise, place the egg yolks, lemon juice, vinegar and cayenne pepper in a food processor and process until smooth. Combine the oils and with the motor still running, slowly drizzle in and process until combined. Season with salt and pepper.

3 To make the pork patties, place all the ingredients in a medium-sized bowl. Using your hands, mix to combine and shape into 12 small, flat, even-sized patties.

4 Preheat a lightly oiled barbecue hotplate or frying pan, then add the patties and cook for 4 minutes on each side, or until cooked through.

5 Drain the vegetables in a sieve and reserve the pickling liquid. Toss the lettuce leaves with a little of the reserved liquid.

6 To assemble, spread the baguettes with mayonnaise. Line with a lettuce leaf and sliced cucumber. Top with patty halves and pickled vegetables. Drizzle with hoisin sauce and scatter with coriander to serve.

SEASON 4 · LUKE & SCOTT

CHICKEN ADOBO TORTILLAS
WITH POMEGRANATE AND LIME SALAD

PREP 30 MINS + MARINATING TIME COOK 15 MINS SERVES 6

8 chicken thighs, cut into 4cm pieces
2 tsp vegetable oil, plus extra, to grease

ADOBO SEASONING

2 tsp chilli powder
1 tsp salt
1 tsp paprika
1 tsp sugar
½ tsp onion powder
¼ tsp garlic powder
¼ tsp cayenne
¼ tsp cumin

COLESLAW

1 tsp honey
juice of 2 limes
½ tsp sea salt
½ red cabbage, shredded
1 cup coriander leaves

CHIMICHURRI

1 cup fresh flat-leaf parsley
2 tbsp oregano leaves
3 cloves garlic, peeled
125ml olive oil
2 tbsp white wine vinegar
1 tsp sea salt
¼ tsp freshly ground black pepper
¼ tsp chilli flakes

TORTILLAS

2 cups plain flour
½ tsp baking powder
½ tsp salt
60g cold butter
250ml warm water

POMEGRANATE AND LIME SALAD

1 tbsp olive oil
1 tbsp lime juice
2 cups baby rocket leaves
½ red onion, peeled and thinly sliced
1 avocado, peeled, deseeded and sliced
seeds of 1 pomegranate

1. To make the adobo seasoning, place all the ingredients in a small bowl and stir to combine. Add the chicken and oil and toss to combine. Cover and refrigerate for 3 hours or overnight.
2. To make the coleslaw, place the honey, lime juice and salt in a large bowl and stir until combined. Stir in the cabbage. Cover and refrigerate for 1 hour, then stir in the coriander.
3. To make the *chimichurri*, place the herbs and garlic in a food processor and process until finely chopped. Stir in the remaining ingredients.
4. To make the tortillas, process the flour, baking powder, salt and butter in a food processor until coarse crumbs form. With the motor running, add the water until a soft dough forms. Divide into 12 portions for small tortillas and 6 portions for large tortillas. Using a rolling pin, roll the portions into thin rounds.
5. Grease a barbecue hotplate or chargrill pan with vegetable oil and place over medium heat. Add the tortillas and cook for 12 minutes on each side, or until golden and crisp. If they puff during cooking, poke a hole to release steam.
6. Add the chicken to the hotplate or pan and cook for 5 minutes, or until browned all over and cooked through.
7. To make the salad, place all the ingredients in a medium bowl and toss to combine.
8. Divide the tortillas among serving plates. Spoon the chicken along the centre of each tortilla. Drizzle *chimichurri* on top, then layer with coleslaw and salad and serve.

WAGYU BEEF CARPACCIO

PREP 45 MINS + REFRIGERATION TIME   COOK 10 MINS   SERVES 4

300g Wagyu beef
200ml olive oil
1 chorizo sausage, thinly sliced
1 celeriac, peeled and julienned
vegetable oil, for deep-frying
1 tbsp baby capers
2 tbsp extra-virgin olive oil
¼ cup shaved Parmesan

MAYONNAISE

2 egg yolks
1 tsp white vinegar
1 tbsp lemon juice
1 tsp Dijon mustard
200ml vegetable oil
salt and pepper, to taste

rocket or micro herbs, to serve

1. Wrap the Wagyu beef in cling film and refrigerate for 30 minutes. Thinly slice.
2. Meanwhile, to make the mayonnaise, process the egg yolks, vinegar, lemon juice and mustard in a food processor until well combined. With the motor running, gradually add the oil, drop by drop at first, then in a thin, steady stream until thick and emulsified. Season with salt and pepper.
3. Place the celeriac in a medium bowl and add just enough mayonnaise to coat. Stir to combine.
4. Preheat a medium frying pan over medium heat. Add the olive oil and chorizo and cook for 5 minutes, or until softened. Process the oil and chorizo in a food processor until well combined, then strain. Reserve the oil.
5. Fill a small saucepan one-third full with vegetable oil and heat over medium heat to 180°C (or until a cube of bread turns golden in 10 seconds). Deep-fry the capers for 1–2 minutes, or until crisp. Remove with a slotted spoon and drain on paper towel.
6. Divide the beef slices and celeriac mixture (*remoulade*) among serving plates. Top with Parmesan and capers and drizzle with chorizo oil and serve with rocket or micro herbs.

Refrigerating the beef prior to cutting will help keep it firm and make it easier to slice thinly. Use the sharpest knife possible to cut the beef. We used a super-sharp sashimi knife.

The marinating time of the scallops in the lime juice is important – any longer and the scallops will 'overcook' and lose their soft, creamy texture.

SCALLOP CEVICHE

PREP 30 MINS COOK 15 MINS SERVES 6

4 small or 2 medium corn cobs
9 large Hervey Bay scallops, halved horizontally
juice of 5 limes, strained
1 large red capsicum, deseeded and diced
1 red onion, peeled and diced, soaked in water for 5 minutes then drained
1 tbsp honey
1 bunch chives, chopped
salt and pepper, to taste

AVOCADO PURÉE

4 small or 2 medium avocados, peeled, deseeded and flesh scooped
4 tbsp olive oil
juice of 2½ limes
2 tsp Tabasco sauce

micro herbs, to garnish

1 Preheat a chargrill pan over medium–high heat. Add the corn cobs and cook, turning, for 15 minutes, or until tender. Set aside to cool for 10 minutes, then remove the kernels from the cobs.

2 Place the scallops in a single layer in a shallow bowl. Pour over the lime juice and refrigerate for 5 minutes.

3 Combine the corn, capsicum, onion, honey and chives in a medium-sized bowl. Season with salt and pepper.

4 To make the avocado purée, process all ingredients in a food processor until smooth and well combined.

5 Brush the avocado purée onto serving plates. Top with the scallops and salsa. Dot the remaining purée onto plates. Garnish with micro herbs.

GOAT'S CHEESE CROQUETTES

WITH ROCKET AND APPLE SALAD AND CARAMELISED MACADAMIAS

PREP 30 MINS COOK 10 MINS SERVES 4

240g goat's cheese
2 tbsp finely chopped macadamia nuts
salt and pepper, to taste
plain flour, for dusting
1 large egg, beaten
1 cup panko breadcrumbs
peanut or vegetable oil, for deep-frying

CARAMELISED MACADAMIAS

¼ cup caster sugar
1 tbsp water
½ cup macadamia nuts

SALAD

1 tbsp lemon juice
1 tbsp olive oil
120g baby rocket leaves
1 apple, cored and julienned

honey, to drizzle

1. To make the croquettes, combine the cheese and nuts in a bowl and season to taste. Divide the mixture into 8 equal portions and roll each portion into a croquette shape.
2. Dust each croquette one at a time in the flour, then dip in the egg and finally the breadcrumbs.
3. Arrange the croquettes in a single layer on a tray lined with baking paper, making sure they don't touch each other. Refrigerate, uncovered, for about 30 minutes, or until firm.
4. Meanwhile, to make the caramelised macadamias, stir the sugar and water in a small, heavy-based frying pan over medium–high heat until the sugar dissolves. Add the nuts. Cook, stirring constantly, until the sugar crystallises and coats the nuts. Transfer the nuts onto a tray lined with baking paper in a single layer to cool and then chop roughly.
5. To make the salad, whisk the lemon juice and olive oil in a large bowl and season to taste. Add the rocket and apple and toss to combine.
6. Deep-fry the croquettes until golden and crisp. Drain on paper towel.
7. Drizzle the croquettes with honey and serve on the salad with caramelised macadamias.

Japanese panko breadcrumbs give a super-crisp result when deep-fried. You can find them in the Asian section of your supermarket.

Garnish the tarts with cracked black pepper and fresh thyme sprigs for added presentation and flavour, if you like.

BEETROOT TART
WITH GOAT'S CHEESE MOUSSE AND BALSAMIC REDUCTION

PREP 30 MINS + 1 HOUR 15 MINS CHILLING COOK 1 HOUR 20 MINS SERVES 4

melted butter, to grease
120g baby rocket leaves
2 tsp olive oil
2 tsp lemon juice
salt and pepper, to taste

BALSAMIC REDUCTION

500ml balsamic vinegar
125ml honey

PASTRY

200g plain flour, plus extra, to dust
100g chilled, unsalted butter, chopped
1 tsp thyme leaves
a pinch of salt

GOAT'S CHEESE MOUSSE

125g cream cheese, softened
50g goat's cheese, crumbled
1 tsp gelatine

BEETROOT FILLING

200g beetroot, peeled and halved
15g unsalted butter
1 tbsp olive oil
1 red onion, peeled and thinly sliced
30ml balsamic vinegar
1 tsp fresh thyme
1 tsp caster sugar

1 To make the balsamic reduction, stir the vinegar and honey in a small saucepan over low–medium heat until the honey has melted. Simmer, stirring frequently, for 20 minutes, or until reduced to 2 cups.

2 To make the pastry, process all ingredients in a food processor until the mixture resembles crumbs. Add 50ml iced water and process until the mixture just comes together. Shape into a disc, wrap in cling film and refrigerate for 30 minutes.

3 Preheat the oven to 180°C. Lightly grease four 10cm round fluted tins with removable bases with melted butter. Divide the pastry into 4 portions. Using a lightly floured rolling pin, roll out each portion on a lightly floured work surface until big enough to line the prepared tins. Ease the pastry into the tins, trimming the excess. Cover the pastry with baking paper and fill with dried beans or rice. Bake for 10 minutes, then remove the beans and paper and bake for a further 5 minutes, or until the base is dry. Set aside to cool.

4 To make the goat's cheese mousse, beat the cream cheese in a medium-sized bowl with a wooden spoon until light and fluffy. Add the goat's cheese and continue beating with a wooden spoon until smooth and combined.

5 In a small saucepan, sprinkle the gelatine over 3 tablespoons cold water. Stand for 1 minute, then stir over low heat until the gelatine has dissolved. Set aside for 10 minutes to cool slightly. Beat the cooled gelatine mixture into the cheese mixture. Pipe or spoon the mixture into four mounds on a tray lined with baking paper. Refrigerate for 45 minutes, or until set.

6 To make the beetroot filling, place the beetroot in a saucepan of cold water over medium heat and bring to the boil. Simmer for 20 minutes, or until just tender. Drain, then set aside to cool. Peel the beetroot, then coarsely grate. Heat the butter and oil in a small frying pan over medium heat. Add the onions and cook, stirring occasionally, for 20 minutes, or until soft. Add the remaining ingredients including the cooled beetroot and cook, stirring, for 5 minutes, or until softened and combined. Season with salt and pepper, then spread the mixture over the tart bases.

7 Divide the tarts between 4 plates and top with the mousse. Drizzle with a little balsamic reduction and serve with the rocket, season with oil, lemon juice, salt and pepper.

SINGAPOREAN CHILLI SOFT SHELL CRAB

PREP 30 MINS + 30 MINS STANDING   COOK 45 MINS   SERVES 4

1 tbsp vegetable oil
2 eschalots, peeled and finely chopped
1cm piece ginger, peeled and finely chopped
4 cloves garlic, peeled and finely chopped
1 tbsp tomato paste
30g toasted peanuts, ground
2 tbsp caster sugar
sesame oil, to brush
vegetable oil, for deep-frying
4 soft shell crabs
rice flour, to dust

REMPAH PASTE

5 bird's-eye chillies, chopped
10 dried chillies, soaked in warm water for 15 minutes then drained, rinsed and roughly chopped
1 tbsp belacan (shrimp paste)
1 stalk lemongrass, white part only, roughly chopped
1cm piece galangal, peeled and chopped
4 candlenuts, toasted

BUNS

200g plain flour, plus extra, to dust
1¾ tsp baking powder
1 tbsp butter
30g caster sugar
¼ tsp white vinegar
sesame oil, to brush

coriander leaves and sliced chilli, to garnish

1 To make the rempah paste, process all the ingredients in a small food processor until finely chopped.

2 Heat the oil in a wok over medium heat. Add the eschalot and ginger and cook, stirring, for 2 minutes, or until fragrant. Stir in the garlic and ¼ cup of the rempah paste, reserving remaining rempah for another use (see note, opposite). Cook, stirring, for 5 minutes, or until softened. Add the tomato paste, peanuts, sugar and 250ml water. Bring to the boil, then simmer for 10 minutes. Cool slightly, then blend the mixture in a food processor until smooth. Set aside.

3 To make the buns, sift the flour and baking powder into the bowl of an electric mixer fitted with a dough hook. Using your fingertips, rub in the butter. Stir in the sugar, then add the vinegar and 60ml lukewarm water. Mix on medium speed until a smooth dough forms. Place the dough in a greased bowl and cover with cling film. Set aside in a warm, draught-free place for 30 minutes.

4 Using lightly floured hands, divide the dough into 4 equal portions. Roll each dough portion into a ball. Line a bamboo steamer with baking paper and brush with sesame oil. Place the dough balls in the steamer and steam, covered, over a saucepan of simmering water for 20 minutes, or until cooked through. Remove from the steamer and set aside for 5 minutes to cool.

5 Fill a deep-fryer or large saucepan one-third full with vegetable oil and heat over medium heat to 180°C (or until a cube of bread turns golden in 10 seconds). Gently drop the buns into the oil and fry, turning halfway, for 3 minutes, or until golden. Remove with a slotted spoon and drain on paper towel, leaving the oil on the heat.

6 Pat the crabs dry with paper towel, then dust in the rice flour. Deep-fry for 2 minutes, or until crisp and golden. Remove with a slotted spoon and drain on paper towel. Cut in half.

7 Place the reserved sauce in a medium frying pan over medium heat and stir for 2 minutes to reheat, adding 60ml warm water to loosen, if necessary. Add the crabs to sauce and stir to coat.

8 Divide the crabs and sauce among 4 plates and garnish with coriander and sliced chilli. Serve with a bun on the side.

Use leftover rempah paste to bring added flavour to your curries and stir-fries.

SEASON 5 · UEL & SHANNELLE

Be patient when cooking the onions as you want the natural sugars to caramelise and become sweet.

PIZZA WITH PEAR, PANCETTA AND ROCKET

PREP 45 MINS + STANDING TIME COOK 40 MINS SERVES 4

100g piece of pancetta, cut into 1cm cubes
50g shaved Parmesan
10 baby bocconcini
1 pear, cored and thinly sliced
100g baby rocket
1 tbsp lemon juice
1 tbsp olive oil
salt and pepper, to taste
50g Gorgonzola, crumbled

PIZZA DOUGH

7g yeast
250ml warm water
275g Italian '00' plain flour
¼ tsp salt
2 tbsp olive oil

CARAMELISED ONIONS

1 tbsp olive oil
1 red onion, peeled and thinly sliced
2 tbsp brown sugar
1 tbsp balsamic vinegar

BALSAMIC GLAZE

125ml balsamic vinegar
55g caster sugar

1 To make the dough, combine the yeast and water in a small bowl. Set aside in a warm place for 10 minutes, or until frothy.
2 Place the flour and salt in the bowl of a mixer fitted with a dough hook. Add the yeast mixture and oil and mix to combine to form a dough.
3 Turn the dough out onto a floured surface and knead until it is smooth and elastic. Place in a greased bowl, cover with a tea towel and set aside in a warm place for 30 minutes, or until doubled in size.
4 Meanwhile, to make the caramelised onions, heat the oil in a frying pan over medium heat. Cook the onion for 2–3 minutes, or until soft and golden brown. Add the sugar and vinegar. Cook, stirring, until the sugar has dissolved and the mixture is thick and dark golden brown. Remove from the heat and cool completely.
5 To make the balsamic glaze, stir the vinegar and sugar in a small saucepan over low heat until the sugar dissolves. Simmer until reduced to a syrup consistency then set aside to cool.
6 Preheat the oven to 220°C. Cook the pancetta in a lightly oiled frying pan over medium heat until lightly browned.
7 Punch the air out of dough and knead until smooth. Roll out on a lightly floured surface until 2mm thick. Place on an oven tray. Top with caramelised onions, Parmesan, bocconcini, pancetta and pear. Bake for about 15 minutes, or until the base is golden and crisp.
8 Toss the rocket with lemon juice, oil and a drizzle of balsamic glaze and season to taste. Top the pizza with rocket and Gorgonzola and serve.

BEETROOT CARPACCIO
WITH CURED SALMON

PREP 1 HOUR 30 MINS COOK 40 MINS SERVES 8–10

1 side fresh salmon, skinned, pin-boned
2 small yellow beetroots
extra-virgin olive oil

BEETROOT CARPACCIO

2 medium red beetroots, peeled
300ml white wine vinegar
300ml water
2 tbsp caster sugar
1 tsp coriander seeds
1 tsp fennel seeds
1 tsp cumin seeds
1 tsp white peppercorns
salt and pepper, to taste

SALT CURING MIXTURE

1kg salt
500g caster sugar
1 tbsp coriander seeds
1 tbsp fennel seeds
1 tbsp cumin seeds
1 tbsp white peppercorns
finely grated zest of 2 lemons

HORSERADISH CREAM

250g crème fraîche,
1 tbsp lemon juice
2 tsp finely grated fresh horseradish

100g jar salmon roe, to serve
baby beetroot leaves and micro herbs, to garnish

1. To make the beetroot carpaccio, place the beetroot in a small saucepan, just large enough to fit. Add the remaining ingredients, ensuring the beetroot is submerged (see note opposite). Partially cover and bring to a gentle boil. Boil for 10–15 minutes, or until tender. Remove the beetroot with a slotted spoon and reserve the cooking liquid.
2. Cool the beetroot and cut into 2mm slices.
3. Simmer the beetroot cooking liquid until reduced to 125ml. Strain and cool. Add the oil and whisk to combine to form a dressing (you may want to add a little more vinegar or sugar to suit your desired taste). Season with salt and pepper.
4. To make the salt curing mixture, combine all ingredients in a bowl. Arrange half the mixture over the base of a rectangular non-reactive dish or pan.
5. Cut the salmon into 3mm-thick slices. Arrange over the salt mixture in a single layer. Top with the remaining salt mixture.
6. Refrigerate, covered, for 40 minutes. Remove the salmon slices and gently rinse in cold water. Pat dry with paper towel. Roll each slice into a round so it will stand up.
7. To make the horseradish cream, combine all ingredients in a bowl. Season to taste and refrigerate until required.
8. Cut the yellow beetroot into 1mm slices. Toss with extra olive oil and season to taste.
9. Arrange the red and yellow beetroot slices on four serving plates and drizzle with dressing. Top with the salmon rolls and dot with salmon roe and horseradish cream. Garnish with beetroot leaves and micro herbs.

The cooking liquid for the beetroot is 50/50 water and vinegar (and is later used to make the dressing). The amount you need may vary depending on the exact size of the beetroot and pan that you use. Increase or decrease, using these ratios, in order to have the beetroot completely submerged during cooking.

MUSHROOM RAVIOLI IN PORCINI BROTH

PREP 50 MINS | COOK 1 HOUR 10 MINS + COOLING | SERVES 8

50g dried porcini mushrooms
250ml dry white wine
2 cloves garlic, peeled and chopped
1 onion, peeled and chopped
1 carrot, peeled and chopped
150g chestnut mushrooms
4 thyme sprigs
1 litre beef stock
2 tsp soy sauce

PASTA

300g Italian '00' flour, plus extra, to dust
½ tsp salt
3 eggs

FILLING

30g butter
1 clove garlic, peeled and crushed
150g mixed wild mushrooms, finely chopped
2 tsp thyme leaves
salt and pepper, to taste

chopped chives or micro herbs, to garnish

1. To make the broth, place mushrooms in a bowl and cover with 375ml hot water. Set aside to soak for 30 minutes.
2. Place the wine in a pressure cooker and simmer until reduced by half. Add the mushrooms with soaking liquid and the remaining broth ingredients. Place the lid on the pressure cooker and bring up to full pressure over high heat. Reduce the heat to low and cook for 1 hour.
3. Release the pressure and remove the lid. Strain the mixture through a fine sieve, discarding the solids.
4. To make the pasta, sift the flour and salt into a large bowl. Make a well in the centre, add the eggs and whisk lightly. Gradually incorporate flour into the centre, adding a little water if necessary, until a soft, pliable dough forms. The dough is the correct consistency if your thumb comes back clean when pushed into it.
5. Knead the dough on a lightly floured work surface for 5 minutes, or until smooth and elastic. Set aside, covered, for 20 minutes to rest.
6. Meanwhile, to make the filling, melt the butter in a frying pan over medium heat. Add the remaining ingredients and cook for 5 minutes, or until softened and the liquid has evaporated. Season with salt and pepper, then cool completely.
7. Divide the pasta into 3 portions. Pass through a pasta machine on the widest setting, repeating on all settings until about 1mm thick.
8. Using an 8cm cutter, cut out 8 rounds from each portion. Place a teaspoon of filling in the centre of each round. Brush the edge with water and fold over to form a half moon.
9. Cook the ravioli in a saucepan of boiling salted water until they float to the surface. Drain.
10. Reheat the broth and divide among serving bowls. Add the ravioli. Garnish with chives to serve.

SCOTCH EGG
WITH HERB MAYONNAISE

PREP 20 MINS COOK 20 MINS SERVES 4

4 whole eggs
1 egg, lightly beaten
400g pork sausage meat
1 tsp ground fennel
1½ tsp English mustard
1½ cups fresh breadcrumbs
salt and pepper, to taste
plain flour, to dust
vegetable oil, for deep-frying

HERB MAYONNAISE

3 egg yolks
2 tsp white wine vinegar
1 tsp lemon juice
250ml light olive oil
2 tsp Dijon mustard
1 tsp finely chopped sage
1 tsp finely chopped parley
1 tsp finely chopped dill

thinly sliced fennel and radish, to serve

1. To make the mayonnaise, process the egg yolks, vinegar and lemon juice in a food processor until well combined. With the motor running, gradually add the oil, drop by drop at first, then in a thin, steady stream until thick and emulsified. Stir in the remaining ingredients and season with salt and pepper. Refrigerate until required.
2. Place 4 eggs in a large saucepan of cold water. Bring to the boil, then boil for 2–3 minutes. Remove and place in iced water to cool completely. Peel.
3. Combine the sausage meat with the fennel, mustard and ¼ cup breadcrumbs. Season with salt and pepper. Divide into 4 portions.
4. Using slightly moistened hands, roll 1 portion into a ball and flatten evenly in the palm of your hand. Place 1 egg in centre and fold in the sausage meat, shaping and moulding to form an even layer around egg. Repeat with the remaining sausage meat and eggs.
5. Preheat the oven to 180°C.
6. Dust the meat-wrapped eggs in flour, dip in the extra egg, allow excess to drain off, then coat in the remaining breadcrumbs. Repeat to form a double layer.
7. Fill a deep-fryer or large saucepan one-third full with the vegetable oil and heat over medium heat to 180°C (or until a cube of bread turns golden in 10 seconds). Gently drop the eggs into the oil and fry, turning halfway, for 2–3 minutes, or until crisp and golden. Remove with a slotted spoon and drain on paper towel.
8. Add to an oven tray and roast for 8–10 minutes, or until extra crisp.
9. Serve the Scotch eggs with the mayonnaise, fennel and radish.

PUMPKIN RAVIOLI
WITH SAGE BUTTER

PREP 35 MINS + 30 MINS RESTING COOK 1 HOUR SERVES 8

450g pumpkin, cut into 4cm pieces
1 tbsp olive oil
¼ tsp fennel seeds, lightly crushed
salt and pepper, to taste
1 egg yolk
25g finely grated Parmesan
1 pinch freshly grated nutmeg
2 amaretti biscuits, crushed
15g fresh white breadcrumbs

PASTA

300g Italian '00' flour, plus extra, to dust
3 eggs
1 tsp salt
2 tsp olive oil

SAGE BUTTER

75g butter
20 sage leaves
1 tbsp lemon juice

toasted pine nuts, to garnish

1. Preheat the oven to 200°C. Place the pumpkin in a roasting tin. Toss with the olive oil and fennel seeds and season with salt and pepper. Roast for 40 minutes, or until tender and lightly caramelised.
2. When cool enough to handle, scoop the flesh away from skin and place in a bowl. Mash lightly with a fork, then stir in the remaining ingredients and season with salt and pepper.
3. To make the pasta, process all the ingredients in a food processor for 10 seconds, or until a crumbly dough forms.
4. Transfer the dough to a lightly floured work surface and knead for 10 minutes, or until smooth and elastic. Cover in cling film and set aside for 30 minutes to rest.
5. Divide the dough into 4 equal portions and keep covered. Using a rolling pin, flatten 1 portion until 5mm thick and about 12cm wide – nearly the width of your pasta machine. Set your pasta machine at its widest setting, then feed the dough through, narrowing the settings on your machine one notch at a time until you reach the thinnest setting. Repeat with the remaining dough.
6. Make small indentations on the dough, 7cm apart and 2cm in from the edge. Place 2 teaspoons of filling on each mark and then brush lines of water between them.
7. Fold over the top half of the dough and, working from the centre of the line outwards, press firmly around each pile of filling with your fingers to push out any trapped air and seal in the filling.
8. Trim off the edges, then cut between rows with a sharp knife or a fluted pasta wheel to make 12 ravioli. Repeat with the remaining dough to make 48 ravioli.
9. To make the sage butter, melt the butter in a large frying pan until foaming. Add the sage and cook, stirring, until golden. Remove from the heat and stir through the lemon juice. Season with salt and pepper.
10. Cook the pasta in batches in a large saucepan of boiling salted water for 1–2 minutes, or until *al dente*. Drain well.
11. Divide the ravioli among 8 plates and spoon over the sage butter. Scatter over toasted pine nuts and serve.

PRAWN CAKES
WITH PEANUT AND LIME DIPPING SAUCE

PREP 40 MINS   COOK 15 MINS   SERVES 4

250g boneless white fish fillets, roughly chopped
500g green prawns, peeled, deveined and roughly chopped
2 tbsp fish sauce
1 tsp rice flour
1 egg
2 spring onions, trimmed and thinly sliced
4 kaffir lime leaves, spine removed, roughly chopped
2 tbsp vegetable oil

RED CURRY PASTE

2 tsp coriander seeds, roasted
1 tsp cumin seeds, roasted
2 tsp white peppercorns
½ tsp ground mace
15 dried red chillies, soaked in hot water for 30 minutes, deseeded and roughly chopped
2 eschalots, peeled and roughly chopped
12 garlic gloves, peeled
2 lemongrass stalks, white part only, chopped
1cm piece galangal, peeled and chopped
4 coriander roots, chopped
1 tbsp finely grated lime zest
2 tsp salt
2 tsp shrimp paste, roasted

PEANUT AND LIME DIPPING SAUCE

110g caster sugar
juice of 2 limes
2 tbsp fish sauce
1 long red chilli, thinly sliced
½ Lebanese cucumber, deseeded and finely diced
2 tbsp finely chopped roasted peanuts

1 To make the curry paste, grind the coriander, cumin and peppercorns to a paste using a mortar and pestle. Place in a food processor with the remaining ingredients and process until a smooth paste forms.

2 Place the fish, prawns, fish sauce, flour and egg in the food processor with the curry paste. Process to combine, then transfer the mixture to a bowl. Using a large metal spoon, mix in the onion and lime leaves.

3 Using wet hands, divide the mixture into 12 equal portions, then shape each into 1cm-thick patties.

4 Heat the oil in a medium frying pan over medium heat. Cook the patties in batches for 2–3 minutes on each side, or until golden. Remove with a slotted spoon and drain on paper towel.

5 To make the dipping sauce, stir the sugar and 60ml water in a small saucepan for 1–2 minutes, or until the sugar dissolves. Cool, then stir in remaining ingredients.

6 Serve the prawn cakes with dipping sauce on the side.

GREEN PAPAYA SALAD
WITH SALT AND PEPPER PRAWNS

PREP 40 MINS COOK 10 MINS SERVES 4

12 medium green prawns, peeled, tails intact
vegetable oil, for deep-frying

SALAD DRESSING

60ml fish sauce
60ml vinegar
2 tbsp grated palm sugar
1 tbsp lime juice

SPICE MIX

½ tsp ground Sichuan pepper
1½ tsp sea salt flakes
1 long red chilli, finely chopped
3 sprigs Vietnamese mint, shredded

GREEN PAPAYA SALAD

500g green papaya, peeled and julienned
2 carrots, peeled and julienned
1 cup shredded mint leaves
1 cup Vietnamese mint
1 cup coriander leaves
½ cup Thai basil leaves

TEMPURA BATTER

225g tempura flour
180g rice flour
400ml cold soda water
juice of 1 lime
1 egg, lightly beaten
1 cup ice cubes

fried eschalots and chopped roasted peanuts, to garnish
lemon wedges, to serve

1 To make the salad dressing, whisk all the ingredients in a bowl until sugar dissolves. Set aside.

2 To make the spice mix, combine all the ingredients in a large bowl.

3 To make the green papaya salad, place all the ingredients in a bowl.

4 To make the tempura batter, sift the flours into a mixing bowl. Using chopsticks, gently stir in the soda water, lime juice and egg until a thin batter forms (it will still have some small lumps). Stir in the ice cubes.

5 Fill a deep-fryer or large saucepan one-third full with vegetable oil and heat over medium heat to 180°C (or until a cube of bread turns golden in 10 seconds). Dip the prawns into the batter, then gently drop into the oil and fry, turning halfway, for 3 minutes, or until crisp and golden. Remove with a slotted spoon and drain on paper towel. Add the prawns to the spice mix and toss to coat.

6 Add the dressing to the salad and toss to combine. Divide the salad among 4 plates and top with the prawns. Garnish with fried eschalots and nuts and serve with lemon wedges on the side.

GRILLED SCAMPI
WITH SAMBAL BEANS

PREP 35 MINS COOK 30 MINS SERVES 4

8 scampi, split lengthways
salt and pepper, to taste
olive oil, for brushing

SAMBAL BEANS

20g dried shrimp
1 tsp belacan (dried shrimp paste)
3 eschalots, peeled and chopped
2 long red chillies, chopped
2 cloves garlic, peeled and crushed
1 tbsp peanut oil
400g green beans, trimmed
250ml water
2 tbsp coconut milk
2 tsp caster sugar

lime wedges, to serve

1 To make the sambal, soak the dried shrimp in cold water for 30 minutes. Drain. Place the belacan in a small, dry frying pan over low heat and cook, stirring, for 2 minutes or until fragrant. Transfer to a small food processor with the eschalots, chillies, garlic and shrimp. Process to form a paste.
2 Heat the oil in a wok over low–medium heat. Cook the paste, stirring, for about 10 minutes, or until soft and fragrant. (If the paste begins to stick, add a little water.) Add the beans and the water.
3 Cook, stirring occasionally, for about 10 minutes, or until the beans are tender. Stir in the coconut milk and sugar.
4 Brush the scampi with oil and season to taste. Cook under a hot grill for about 3 minutes, or until just cooked.
5 Serve the scampi with sambal beans and lime wedges on the side.

We cooked the scampi separately, however you could chargrill the scampi flesh-side down for 2 minutes, then finish cooking for a further 1–2 minutes (depending on the size of the scampi) with the sambal beans for a more infused flavour.

The key to cooking liver is to achieve a sealed, browned exterior while keeping the centre pink and moist.

SEASON 6 · JAC & SHAZ

CHICKEN LIVERS
WITH PORT AND PROSCIUTTO

PREP 40 MINS + 1 HOUR STANDING   COOK 40 MINS   SERVES 4

50g butter
1 tbsp olive oil
2 large brown onions, peeled and thinly sliced
salt and pepper, to taste
4 slices prosciutto
500g chicken livers, trimmed
80ml port

CRUSTY BREAD

450ml warm water
2 tbsp caster sugar
7g sachet instant dry yeast
600g bread flour
2 tsp salt
4 cups ice cubes
olive oil, for brushing

1 green apple, julienned, to garnish
chopped parsley or micro herbs, to garnish

1. To make the bread, stir the warm water, sugar and yeast in the bowl of an electric mixer until the yeast dissolves. Set aside in a warm place for 10 minutes, or until frothy. Sift the flour and salt into the bowl over the frothy yeast mixture. Using a dough hook, mix on the lowest speed until combined. Increase the speed to medium and mix for 5 minutes, or until the dough is smooth and elastic.
2. Turn the dough out onto a floured surface and divide into 4 portions. Roll each portion into a 3cm thick sausage. Plait 2 of the lengths to form 1 loaf. Repeat with the remaining lengths. Place on a tray lined with baking paper and set aside in a warm place for 1 hour, or until doubled in size.
3. Meanwhile, preheat the oven to 220°C. Place a deep tray on the base of the oven (for the ice). When the dough is ready, working quickly, place the tray in the oven and immediately pour the ice cubes into the tray on the base of the oven.
4. Bake for 25 minutes or until golden, crusty and the loaf sounds hollow when tapped. Remove from the oven and transfer to a wire rack to cool. Slice thickly.
5. To caramelise the onions, heat half the butter and oil in a deep frying pan over medium heat. Cook the onions, stirring occasionally, for 3–5 minutes, or until dark golden brown. Season to taste, remove from the pan and set aside.
6. Add the prosciutto to the same pan and cook until crisp.
7. Rinse the chicken livers and pat dry with paper towel. Season all over. Heat the remaining butter and oil in the same frying pan over medium–high heat until foaming. Add the livers and cook for 30 seconds on each side, or until browned but still pink in the middle. Transfer to a warm plate.
8. Return the onions to the pan and add the port to deglaze. Simmer until almost evaporated, stirring to remove any sticky sediment on the base of the pan. Season to taste, return the livers to the pan and toss to combine.
9. Brush the bread slices with oil, season to taste and cook on a hot chargrill on both sides until toasted. Serve the liver and onions topped with prosciutto. Garnish with apple and parsley or micro herbs and serve with the bread.

PRAWNS, AVOCADO AND PINK GRAPEFRUIT

PREP 1 HOUR 30 MINS   COOK 20 MINS   SERVES 4

400g green prawns, heads and tails removed and reserved
1 pink grapefruit, peeled and segmented
½ small Lebanese cucumber, deseeded and cut into 5mm dice
salt and pepper, to taste
2 large avocados
lemon juice, for brushing

LIME AND DILL CREAM

150g crème fraîche
2 tbsp finely chopped dill
1 tbsp lime juice
2 tsp finely grated lime zest

PRAWN OIL

125ml olive oil
100g prawn heads and tails (from above)
1 tsp tomato paste

PRAWN POACHING LIQUID

250ml white wine
500ml water
6 black peppercorns
2 bay leaves
1 lemon, halved
1 tbsp salt

micro herbs, to garnish
large salmon roe, to garnish

1. To make the lime and dill cream, whisk all the ingredients in a bowl to combine and season to taste.
2. To make the prawn oil, heat the oil in a saucepan over medium heat. Cook the prawn heads and tails, lightly pounding with a wooden spoon or rolling pin, until crisp. Stir in the tomato paste. Cook, stirring, for 2 minutes. Simmer over the lowest heat until the flavour and colour have intensified, and season to taste. Cool completely, then strain and discard the solids.
3. To make the poaching liquid, bring all the ingredients to the boil in a large saucepan. Simmer for 10 minutes, then add the prawns and simmer, covered, for 2 minutes, or until almost cooked. Turn off the heat, stand for 1 minute, or until just cooked. Drain and cut into 1cm-thick pieces.
4. Coarsely chop half the grapefruit segments and add to the prawns with the cucumber and enough lime and dill cream to lightly coat. Season to taste.
5. Halve one avocado, remove the pip and peel. Thinly cut 1 avocado half into slices, brushing with lemon juice as you go, to prevent browning. Arrange the slices, overlapping in a row, on a large rectangle of baking paper.
6. Spoon a quarter of the prawn filling along the centre of the row. Using the baking paper as a guide, gently roll the avocado to enclose the filling. Twist the ends of the baking paper to secure and refrigerate for 10 minutes, or until firm. Repeat with the remaining avocado and filling.
7. Remove the paper from the avocado rolls and trim the ends.
8. Divide the avocado rolls among 4 serving plates. Season to taste, add a spoonful of the lime and dill cream and dot with prawn oil. Garnish with micro herbs, salmon roe and the remaining grapefruit segments.

The slices of avocado will need to be fairly uniform in size to make the roll/roulade, so you may find you only use the pieces that span the length of the fruit.

ZUCCHINI AND POTATO RÖSTI STACK
WITH SMOKED SALMON AND CRÈME FRAÎCHE

PREP 25 MINS COOK 20 MINS SERVES 4

3 tbsp vegetable oil, for frying
200g crème fraîche
1 tbsp lemon juice
1 tbsp finely chopped dill
100g rocket leaves
200g sliced smoked salmon

RÖSTI

300g zucchini, trimmed and coarsely grated
2 tsp salt
250g potatoes, peeled and coarsely grated
2 eggs, lightly beaten
75g plain flour
2 tbsp finely chopped chives
salt and pepper, to taste

baby capers and olive oil, to serve

1 To make the rösti, place the zucchini in a sieve over a bowl. Stir through half the salt. Stand for 10 minutes to drain then push down to remove excess liquid. Transfer to a clean bowl and set aside. Repeat with the potato.

2 Combine the zucchini, potato and remaining ingredients in a large bowl. Season with salt and pepper.

3 Heat the oil in a large non-stick frying pan over medium heat. Take ¼ cup of the mixture and lightly press into three 8cm circles in the pan. Cook for 2–3 minutes on each side, or until golden, crisp and cooked through. Remove with a slotted spoon and drain on paper towel. Repeat with the remaining mixture to make 12 rösti.

4 Combine the crème fraîche, lemon juice and dill in a small bowl. Season with salt and pepper.

5 Place 1 rösti on each of 4 plates. Divide a third of the rocket among each rösti, then repeat with the salmon and then the crème fraîche mixture to make a stack. Repeat twice more, ending with crème fraîche mixture. Top with capers, then drizzle over oil to serve.

MKR
MY KITCHEN RULES

MAINS

HANDMADE SICILIAN PORK AND FENNEL SAUSAGES

WITH CREAMY LEEK MASH

PREP 1 HOUR + 1 HOUR REFRIGERATION COOK 1 HOUR 20 MIN SERVES 4

3kg deboned pork shoulder, skin and fat on
1 tsp fennel seeds
sea salt and freshly ground black pepper, to taste
½ tsp dried chilli flakes
medium sausage casing, washed in salted water
1 radicchio lettuce, washed and sliced into thin wedges

ROASTED TOMATOES

12 small truss tomatoes, still on stem
4 cloves garlic, unpeeled
1 tbsp olive oil

LEEK MASH

500g Desiree potatoes, peeled and cut into small cubes
milk, to cover
1 bay leaf
½ leek, white part only, roughly chopped
50g butter

DRESSING

2 tbsp olive oil
juice of ¼ lemon
1 tbsp red wine vinegar

lemon wedges, to serve

1 Remove the fat from the pork skin. Discard the skin and cut the fat and pork into small dice. Feed through a mincer on a large/coarse setting. Combine the mince with the fennel seeds, salt, pepper and chilli to form the sausage meat.

2 Using an electric sausage maker, fill the casings with sausage meat. Twirl the sausage onto itself in a snail-like shape to create 4 rounds. Secure each round through the centre with a bamboo skewer (it should look like an old-fashioned lollipop). Refrigerate, covered, for 1 hour.

3 Preheat the oven to 150°C. Place the tomatoes and garlic cloves on a tray lined with baking paper, drizzle with oil and season with salt and pepper. Cook for 45 minutes, or until very tender but still whole.

4 To make the leek potato mash, bring the potatoes, milk, bay leaf and leek to the boil in a medium-sized saucepan. Simmer until the potato and leek are tender. Drain and discard the leek and bay leaf, reserving the milk. Pass the potato through a fine sieve. Stir in the butter and some of the reserved milk. Season to taste and cover to keep warm.

5 To make the dressing, whisk all the ingredients together in a large bowl. Add the radicchio and toss to combine.

6 Heat a grill pan over high heat. Add the sausage rounds and cook for 3–4 minutes on each side, or until browned and cooked through.

7 Divide the mash over 4 plates and top with a sausage. Place the roasted tomatoes and garlic on the side along with a generous portion of radicchio salad. Garnish with a wedge of fresh lemon and serve immediately.

Sausage casing is available from your local butcher. The great thing about homemade sausages is that you can experiment with flavours. Try adding your favourite spice or herb, a little citrus rind or chopped olives and sun-dried tomatoes.

Salting the eggplant draws out any bitter juices. Marinated anchovies have been preserved in vinegar. They have a much milder flavour than the anchovies in jars that have been cured/salted. They are available from delicatessens.

SEASON 1 · VERONICA & SHADI

GRILLED SWORDFISH
WITH EGGPLANT AND ANCHOVIES

PREP 45 MIN COOK 40 MIN SERVES 4

2 medium eggplants, trimmed and cut into 2cm pieces
2 tbsp sea salt
1 tbsp olive oil, plus extra for brushing
125ml white vinegar
½ tbsp finely chopped parsley
½ tbsp finely chopped fresh mint
4 x 200g swordfish fillets
4 white marinated anchovies

EGGPLANT MARINADE

1 fresh long red chilli, finely chopped
3 cloves garlic, peeled and finely chopped
zest and juice of 1 lemon
½ tbsp finely chopped fresh oregano
8 fresh sage leaves, chopped
freshly ground white pepper, to taste
60ml olive oil

fresh herbs and lemon wedges, to garnish

1 Place the eggplant in a large bowl and generously sprinkle with sea salt. Stand for at least 20 minutes before rinsing away the excess salt.

2 Pat the eggplant dry with paper towel and combine with the marinade ingredients in a large bowl. Marinate for at least 20 minutes, then drain the eggplant and reserve the marinade.

3 Heat the oil in a large, heavy-based frying pan over medium heat. Add the eggplant and cook, stirring occasionally, for 1–2 minutes. Add the vinegar and the marinade. Cook for a further 10 minutes, stirring occasionally, until the eggplant is golden brown and tender. Stir in the parsley and mint.

4 Heat a large grill pan. Brush the fish with oil and season with salt and pepper. Cook on one side for 2–3 minutes, then turn and cook for a further minute.

5 To serve, divide the eggplant over 4 plates and top with anchovies and swordfish. Garnish with fresh herbs and lemon wedges and serve immediately.

SALMON FISH FINGERS
WITH COLD SOBA NOODLES

PREP 1 HOUR COOK 20 MINS SERVES 4

½ x 300g packet soba noodles
2 spring onions, trimmed and thinly sliced
vegetable oil, for deep-frying

SALMON

1 tbsp water
1 tbsp white miso paste
400g salmon fillets, skinned and boned, cut into fingers
1 egg, beaten lightly
100g panko breadcrumbs
3 tbsp sesame seeds

MENTSUYU DRESSING

75ml dark soy sauce
2 tsps caster sugar
2 tsp mirin
dashi stock powder (to make 500ml)
1 tbsp bonito flakes

PICKLED CARROTS

100ml water
100ml rice wine vinegar
55g caster sugar
2 carrots, peeled and cut into matchsticks

Japanese kewpie mayonnaise, to serve

1 To prepare the salmon, combine the water and miso in a large bowl. Add the salmon and toss to coat. Cover and refrigerate until required.

2 To make the *mentsuyu* dressing, stir the soy, sugar and mirin in a small saucepan until the sugar dissolves.

3 Make 500ml dashi stock in a small saucepan, according to packet instructions. Add the bonito flakes and simmer gently for 5 minutes. Strain and discard the bonito flakes. Add the *mentsuyu* dressing to the strained dashi.

4 To make the pickled carrots, stir the water, vinegar and sugar in a small saucepan over low heat until the sugar has dissolved. Bring to the boil and add the carrots. Boil for 30 seconds, or until just tender. Drain.

5 Cook the noodles in a large saucepan of boiling water until just tender. Drain and transfer to a bowl of iced water to stop the cooking process. Drain and place in a bowl with the carrots, spring onions and two-thirds of the *mentsuyu* dressing.

6 To continue preparing the salmon, place the egg in a small bowl and combine the breadcrumbs and sesame seeds in another bowl. Dip the salmon fingers in the egg, then the breadcrumb mixture.

7 Heat the oil to 180°C (or until a cube of bread turns golden in 10 seconds). Deep-fry the salmon fingers until golden brown, then drain on paper towel.

8 Divide the noodles among 4 bowls and top with the salmon fingers. Serve with mayonnaise and the remaining *mentsuyu* dressing for dipping.

Bonito flakes are dried, smoked flakes of bonito fish (a type of tuna), available in Japanese/Asian supermarkets. We cut our salmon into 2cm × 10cm fingers.

We cooked our asparagus in a vacuum-sealed bag to preserve maximum flavour. To do this, place asparagus, one sliced garlic clove, salt, pepper and a dash of olive oil in a vacuum bag. Seal and poach in simmering water for 5 minutes.

PAN-FRIED BLUE-EYE TREVALLA
WITH CARAMELISED FENNEL

PREP 30 MINS   COOK 40 MINS   SERVES 4

4 x 80g fillets blue-eye trevalla
1½ tbsp extra-virgin olive oil
2 tsp butter
12 baby asparagus spears

CARAMELISED FENNEL

25g butter
2 tsp olive oil
1 small fennel bulb, trimmed and thinly sliced
1 small onion, peeled and thinly sliced
2 tsp caster sugar
1 tbsp verjuice
2 tsps white wine vinegar
salt and pepper, to taste

PARSLEY AND ANCHOVY SAUCE

½ bunch parsley, finely chopped
1 clove garlic, peeled and crushed
3 salted anchovies, rinsed and finely chopped
60ml extra-virgin olive oil
juice of ½ lemon

1 To make the caramelised fennel, heat the butter and oil in a medium-sized frying pan. Add the fennel and onion and cook, over low heat, for 30 minutes, stirring occasionally, until soft and caramelised. Stir in the sugar and verjuice halfway through cooking. Stir in the vinegar and season with salt and pepper to taste.

2 To make the parsley and anchovy sauce, blend all the ingredients until smooth.

3 Season the fish all over. Heat half the olive oil in a medium-sized frying pan over medium heat. Add the fish, skin-side down, and cook for 5 minutes, or until the skin is crisp and the fish is cooked two-thirds of the way through. Add the butter. Turn the fish and cook for a further minute.

4 Meanwhile, steam the asparagus until tender. Drizzle with the remaining oil and season to taste.

5 To serve, top a spoonful of the fennel with fish. Serve with the asparagus and sauce.

BEEF SUKIYAKI

PREP 4 HOURS + OVERNIGHT REFRIGERATION   COOK 45 MINUTES   SERVES 4

1 cup finely sliced wombok
50g shiitake mushrooms, thinly sliced
125g Wagyu beef fillet
¼ roll of *naruto maki*
¼ x 200g punnet enoki mushrooms
salt and pepper, to taste
125g bean thread noodles
½ x 225g can bamboo shoots, drained
1 spring onion, thinly sliced

BEEF STOCK

500g beef shin
1kg beef bones, with marrow
4 cloves garlic
1 tbsp peanut oil
1 leek, chopped
1 carrot, chopped
1 onion, peeled and chopped
1cm piece fresh ginger, peeled and sliced
2 bay leaves
1 tsp black peppercorns
3 litres water

DASHI STOCK

250ml cold water
5g kombu
1 tbsp bonito flakes

SUKIYAKI BROTH

1 litre beef stock (see above)
60ml dashi stock (see above)
60ml soy sauce
60ml sake
1 tbsp mirin
2 tsp sesame oil

4 eggs, to serve

1 To make the beef stock, preheat the oven to 180°C. Place the beef shin, beef bones and garlic in a roasting pan and roast for 20 minutes or until browned.

2 Heat the peanut oil in a stockpot over medium heat. Add the vegetables and cook, stirring occasionally, for 5 minutes. Add the roasted beef shin, beef bones and garlic (skin removed) with the remaining ingredients and bring to the boil. Simmer, uncovered, for 2 hours, or until reduced to 1 litre. Cool and refrigerate overnight.

3 Skim off solidified fat, strain and discard the solids. Place the stock in a saucepan and bring to a simmer.

4 To make the dashi stock, bring the water and kombu to a fast simmer. Just before the boil, remove the kombu and add the bonito flakes. Remove from the heat and allow to stand for 5 minutes, or until the bonito flakes have sunk to the bottom of the pan. Strain and discard the flakes.

5 To make the sukiyaki broth, bring all the ingredients to a simmer in a large saucepan. Season to taste.

6 Heat a lightly oiled frying pan over low–medium heat. Stir-fry the wombok and mushrooms separately until just soft. Season to taste, remove from the pan and set aside.

7 Increase the heat, season the Wagyu beef and cook for about 1 minute on each side until seared and browned. Remove from the pan and rest for 5 minutes. Slice very thinly.

8 Slice the *naruto maki* into 5mm rounds and cook in a saucepan of boiling, salted water for 1 minute. Remove with a slotted spoon and drain on paper towel. Add the noodles to the boiling water for 2 minutes, or until tender, using a fork to separate them. Drain and rinse under cold water.

9 Divide the noodles among 4 bowls. Top with the wombok, mushrooms, *naruto maki*, bamboo shoots and spring onion. Arrange the beef on top of the vegetables and pour over the boiling broth. Serve each bowl with a raw egg to stir through.

You can use any other noodles in place of the bean thread noodles. Soba noodles and udon noodles make a great substitute. Traditionally sukiyaki is cooked or simmered at the table in a shallow iron pot with the beef served on the side and dragged through the broth to cook.

For extra crispy crackling, sprinkle the rind with salt and refrigerate, uncovered, overnight. This draws the moisture out. Wipe dry before cooking.
SEASON 3 · ANGELA & JUSTINE

PROSCIUTTO, APPLE AND GORGONZOLA PORK CHOPS
WITH ASPARAGUS AND PEA RISOTTO

PREP 30 MINS COOK 60 MINS SERVES 4

24cm piece pork rind
1 tbsp vegetable oil
salt, to season
4 pork loin chops, frenched
8 sage leaves
1 Granny Smith apple, cored and thinly sliced into rounds
40g Gorgonzola, sliced
4 slices prosciutto

RISOTTO

1 tbsp olive oil
35g butter, chopped
½ onion, peeled and finely chopped
1 celery stick, finely chopped
150g arborio rice
125ml dry white wine
600ml hot chicken stock
salt and pepper, to taste
½ bunch asparagus, cut into 1cm pieces
65g frozen peas
40g grated Parmesan
zest and juice of ½ lemon

1 Preheat the oven to 200°C. Brush the pork rind with oil and season with salt, then place, skin-side up, on a rack over a baking tray and cook for 50–60 minutes, or until small bubbles form on surface and the rind is golden and crisp.

2 Meanwhile, heat a lightly oiled frying pan over high heat. Cook the pork chops in 2 batches for 2 minutes on each side, or until brown. Transfer to an oven tray.

3 Top each chop with 2 sage leaves, 3 apple slices and 10g of the Gorgonzola. Wrap each chop with 1 slice of prosciutto and set aside.

4 To make the risotto, heat the oil and 10g of the butter in a large saucepan over medium heat. Add the onion and celery and cook, stirring occasionally, for 15 minutes, or until soft. Stir in the rice and add the wine. Cook, stirring, until evaporated. Add the hot stock, ½ cup at a time, stirring constantly between additions, until the stock is absorbed. This should take about 20–25 minutes. The rice should be tender and creamy, but not stodgy. Season lightly with salt and pepper. Stir in the asparagus and peas for the last 10 minutes of cooking. Remove from the heat and stir in the Parmesan, lemon zest and juice, as well as the remaining butter.

5 Place the pork in the oven and cook for 10 minutes, or until the prosciutto is crisp and the pork is cooked as desired. Stand, covered, for 5 minutes.

6 Serve pork with the crackling and risotto.

MULLOWAY
WITH CELERIAC PURÉE AND BEURRE ROUGE

PREP 1 HOUR COOK 45 MINS SERVES 4

12 asparagus spears, trimmed and peeled
¼ tsp bicarbonate of soda
15g butter
4 zucchini flowers

CELERIAC PURÉE

500ml milk
500g celeriac, peeled and cut into 2cm pieces
5 sprigs thyme
1 bay leaf
25g butter, diced
salt and pepper, to taste

BEURRE ROUGE

600ml red wine
180ml red wine vinegar
7 eschalots, peeled and finely chopped
7 sprigs thyme
2 bay leaves
1 tsp black peppercorns
a pinch of brown sugar
250g cold unsalted butter, diced

FISH

4 x 150g mulloway fillets, skin-on, pin boned
1 tbsp olive oil
25g butter
4 sprigs thyme

micro herbs, to garnish

1. To make the celeriac purée, place the milk, celeriac and herbs in a medium-sized saucepan. Season to taste and cover with a cartouche. Bring to a simmer and simmer for 30 minutes, or until very tender. Remove and discard the thyme stalks and bay leaf. Strain the celeriac, reserving the milk.
2. Process the celeriac and butter in a food processor until smooth. Add enough of the milk to form a thin purée. Season to taste then push through a fine sieve, twice, into a clean saucepan. Reheat on low heat before serving.
3. Meanwhile, to make the *beurre rouge*, place wine, vinegar, eschalots, thyme, bay leaves, peppercorns and sugar in a medium-sized saucepan. Bring to a simmer and simmer for approximately 25 minutes, until reduced to 150ml.
4. Strain the mixture into a clean saucepan and place over low heat. Whisk in the butter a cube at a time. Season to taste and remove from the heat. Cover to keep warm.
5. Remove the stamens from the zucchini flowers. Cook in a saucepan of boiling water for 10 seconds. Drain and pat dry with paper towel. Trim away the base and cut a slit from top to bottom so you can open the flowers out flat.
6. Score the fish skin at 5mm intervals. Season well. Heat the oil in a frying pan over medium–high heat. Add the butter and thyme, then add the fish, skin-side down. Cook for 5 minutes, or until skin is crisp. Turn and cook for a further 1–2 minutes, or until just cooked through (the fish will continue to cook on standing).
7. Cook the asparagus in boiling water with bicarbonate of soda for 1 minute. Drain, then refresh in iced water and drain again. Melt the butter in a frying pan over medium heat. Add asparagus and season well. Toss over for 30 seconds, or until hot.
8. To serve, place a flattened zucchini flower on each of four plates. Spoon the purée at the base of the flower. Top with fish and asparagus spears. Garnish with micro herbs and serve with *beurre rouge*.

Mulloway is found along the east and south coast of Australia. If mulloway is unavailable, then substitute with blue-eye trevalla, grouper or another firm white fish. The exact cooking time of fish will depend on thickness of fillets.

Try varying the filling of the chicken. Chopped olives, sundried tomatoes or chargrilled antipasto would work well as an addition, instead of the mushrooms.

PROSCIUTTO-WRAPPED CHICKEN
WITH GARLIC MASH AND SNOW PEAS

PREP 20 MINS COOK 45 MINS SERVES 4

4 large chicken thigh fillets, skin-on
1 field mushroom, sliced
4 slices prosciutto
2 cloves garlic, peeled and crushed
2 sprigs rosemary

GARLIC MASH

800g Desiree potatoes, peeled and chopped
salt and pepper, to taste
4 cloves garlic, roasted, skins removed
160ml milk
50g butter, cubed
¼ cup chopped chives

JUS

60ml olive oil
2 brown onions, peeled and chopped
310ml dry white wine
500ml chicken stock

steamed snow peas, to serve

1 To make the prosciutto-wrapped chicken, preheat the oven to 200°C. Place the chicken thighs, skin-side down, on a chopping board and make an incision in the thickest part of the meat to create a pocket, being careful not to cut all the way through. Divide the mushroom slices among the chicken thigh pockets and fold the thigh over to enclose. Wrap each chicken parcel in prosciutto and place, seam-side down, in a greased ovenproof dish. Rub the chicken with garlic and add rosemary to the dish.

2 Roast for 40 minutes, or until cooked through. Remove the chicken from oven, transfer to a plate and cover with foil to keep warm.

3 Meanwhile, to make the garlic mash, place the potatoes in a large saucepan of salted water and bring to the boil, then simmer gently for 15 minutes, or until potatoes are tender. Drain, then mash until smooth. Add roasted garlic, milk, butter and chives and stir to combine. Season with salt and pepper, then cover to keep warm.

4 To make the jus, heat the oil in a medium saucepan. Add the onions and cook over medium heat, stirring occasionally, for 5 minutes or until soft. Add the wine, bring to the boil, then reduce the heat and simmer for 3 minutes, or until reduced by half. Add the stock and simmer, uncovered, for 10 minutes, or until reduced by half, then strain.

5 Slice the chicken into rounds and serve with garlic mash, jus and snow peas.

CAJUN JAMBALAYA

PREP 45 MINS COOK 45–50 MINS SERVES 4

50ml peanut oil
2 chorizos, sliced
4 chicken lovely legs, skin-on
8 large green prawns, peeled, deveined, tails intact and heads reserved
1 celery stick, thinly sliced
½ onion, peeled and thinly sliced
3 cloves garlic, peeled and crushed
1 long red chilli, thinly sliced
3 Roma tomatoes, deseeded and diced
1 pinch of saffron threads, soaked in 1 tbsp boiling water
1 thyme sprig, leaves picked
1 bay leaf
1 litre chicken stock
2 blue swimmer crabs
100g long-grain rice
300g mussels, debearded and cleaned
300g pippies

SPICE MIX

1 tbsp peanut oil
½ onion, peeled and chopped
3 cloves garlic, peeled and crushed
½ tsp cayenne pepper
½ tsp chopped thyme
½ tsp celery salt
½ tsp smoked paprika
½ tsp cracked black pepper
½ tsp sea salt

2 spring onions, trimmed and thinly sliced on the diagonal, to serve

1. Heat 1 tablespoon of the oil in a large frying pan over medium–high heat. Add the chorizo and cook for 4–5 minutes, or until browned. Remove and drain on paper towel. Add the chicken to the pan and cook, turning, until browned on all sides. Remove from the pan and set aside.
2. Heat the remaining oil in the same frying pan. Add the prawn heads and cook over medium heat, stirring, for 5 minutes. Discard the heads, reserving oil. Add the celery, onion, garlic and chilli and fry for 5 minutes. Add tomatoes, saffron mixture, thyme and bay leaf, then cook, stirring, for 5 minutes. Add the stock and bring to a simmer, then add the chicken and chorizo and simmer for 10 minutes, or until the liquid is reduced by one-quarter.
3. Meanwhile, cook the crabs in a large stockpot of salted boiling water for 5 minutes, or until cooked through. Remove and refresh in iced water. Break off the tail flaps on the underside and discard. Cut each crab in half lengthways, then carefully pull off the back shells and discard. Remove the 'dead man's fingers' (soft gills) and discard, then rinse and discard the stomach sac. Set aside.
4. To make the spice mix, heat the oil in a small frying pan over medium heat. Add the onion and garlic and cook for 3 minutes, or until soft. Add the remaining ingredients and cook for a further minute, or until fragrant. Using a mortar and pestle, grind the spices to a paste.
5. Add the spice paste to the chicken mixture, stirring until combined, then add the rice and simmer for 10 minutes.
6. Add the mussels and cook for 3 minutes. Add the prawns and cook for a further 2–3 minutes, then add the crab pieces and pippies and cook for 3–5 minutes, or until cooked through.
7. Spoon the jambalaya into serving bowls and top with spring onions to serve.

Chicken lovely legs are chicken legs that have had the bone trimmed and are available from supermarkets and butchers.

Tamarind water can be made by soaking a piece of tamarind in hot water for 10–15 minutes and then straining off the liquid, discarding any seeds or residue.

MASSAMAN CURRY
WITH ROTI AND PICKLED SALAD

PREP 1 HOUR   COOK 1 HOUR   SERVES 4

5 tbsp grapeseed oil
1.8kg oxtail, cut into pieces at joints
500ml pineapple juice
4 bay leaves
4 Kipfler potatoes, peeled and sliced
12 eschalots, plus 14 extra, peeled and chopped
60ml fish sauce
60ml tamarind water
50g peanuts, roasted

PICKLED SALAD
75g caster sugar
70ml water
70ml white wine vinegar
salt and pepper, to taste
4 Lebanese cucumbers, diced
5 eschalots, peeled and thinly sliced
3 long red chillies, thinly sliced

ROTI
375g plain flour, plus extra, to dust
125ml milk
60ml water
a pinch of salt
2½ tbsp butter, plus extra, to grease
ghee, for frying

coriander leaves, to garnish

PASTE
1 tsp cumin seeds
1 tbsp coriander seeds
1 tsp ground nutmeg
1 stick cassia bark
8 Thai cardamom pods, 4 whole, 4 seeds only
4 cloves
½ tsp ground mace
7 eschalots, peeled
7 cloves garlic, peeled
3 lemongrass stalks, bruised
7 coriander roots
8cm piece galangal, peeled and chopped
4 dried long red chillies, soaked, drained, stalks removed
¼ tsp chilli powder
3 tbsp grapeseed oil
600ml coconut cream

1 Heat 2 tablespoons of oil in a pressure cooker over medium heat. Add the oxtail and cook for 5–8 minutes, or until browned. Add the pineapple juice and bay leaves, bring to the boil and cook, covered, for 50 minutes or until cooked and tender.

2 Meanwhile, to make the pickled salad, combine the sugar, water and vinegar in a small saucepan over medium heat and bring to the boil. Reduce the heat to low and simmer for 5 minutes, or until reduced slightly. Remove from the heat and season with salt and pepper. Cool. Combine the cucumbers, eschalots and chillies in a medium-sized bowl, then toss through the dressing.

3 To make the roti, combine the flour, milk, water, salt and butter in a large bowl until a dough forms. Turn out onto a lightly floured work surface and knead for 5 minutes, or until the dough is smooth and elastic. Place the dough in a greased bowl and cover with cling film. Set aside in a warm, draught-free place for 40 minutes. Divide into 8 portions and roll out with a rolling pin until 5mm thick. Place on an oven tray and set aside.

continued next page ➤

MASSAMAN CURRY

WITH ROTI AND PICKLED SALAD

(continued)

4 Meanwhile, to make the paste, toast the cumin seeds, coriander seeds, nutmeg, cassia bark, cardamom seeds, cloves and mace in a small frying pan over medium heat for 1–2 minutes, or until fragrant. Place the mixture in a mortar and pestle and grind to a powder. Sift into a bowl and set aside.

5 Place the eschalots, garlic, lemongrass, coriander roots and galangal in a small saucepan and dry-fry for 5 minutes, or until fragrant. Transfer to a food processor with the sifted spice mix, chillies, chilli powder and 2 tablespoons of grapeseed oil. Process until smooth.

6 Heat the remaining tablespoon of grapeseed oil in a large saucepan over medium heat. Add the paste and cook for 5 minutes, or until the oil turns a red colour. Gradually add the coconut cream, along with the whole cardamom pods. Cook for 10–15 minutes, or until combined. Add a little water if it's too thick.

7 Uncover the pressure cooker and transfer the oxtail to the curry paste mixture. Skim off fat from the pressure cooker and add 250ml of the cooking liquid to the curry, along with the potatoes and eschalots. Reduce the heat to low and simmer for 10 minutes. Add the fish sauce and tamarind water and simmer for a further 10–15 minutes, or until the potatoes are cooked through. Stir in the peanuts.

8 Meanwhile, heat the remaining 3 tablespoons of oil in a small saucepan over medium–high heat. Add the extra eschalots and cook for 1–2 minutes, or until crispy, then drain on paper towel.

9 Heat a little ghee in a frying pan over medium heat. Cook the roti for 2 minutes on each side, or until golden and puffed.

10 Spoon the curry into 4 serving bowls, top with crispy eschalots and garnish with coriander. Serve with roti and pickled salad.

JERK CHICKEN
WITH COCONUT RICE AND PINEAPPLE SALSA

PREP 35 MINS COOK 1 HOUR SERVES 4

vegetable oil, for frying
4 chicken Marylands, skin-on

MARINADE

2 brown onions, peeled and coarsely chopped
3 spring onions, trimmed and coarsely chopped
6 cloves garlic, peeled and coarsely chopped
6cm piece fresh ginger, peeled and coarsely chopped
2 long red chillies, chopped
2 tsp chilli flakes
1 tbsp ground allspice
1 tbsp dried thyme
1 tsp ground cinnamon
1 tbsp brown sugar
2 tsp ground oregano
½ tbsp cayenne pepper
1½ tsp freshly ground black pepper
1 tsp salt
juice of 1 orange
juice of 1 lime
60ml olive oil
60ml soy sauce

COCONUT RICE

2 tbsp olive oil
1 onion, peeled and finely chopped
1 red long chilli, deseeded and finely chopped
2 cloves garlic, peeled and crushed
400g long-grain rice, rinsed
400ml coconut milk
240ml water
60ml chicken stock
salt and pepper, to taste
400g can kidney beans, drained

PINEAPPLE SALSA

½ small pineapple, peeled and cut into 5mm dice
1 Lebanese cucumber, deseeded and finely diced
1 small red onion, peeled and finely diced
juice of 1 lime
2 tsp honey

YOGHURT SAUCE

300g Greek yoghurt
½ bunch coriander, finely chopped
½ bunch mint, finely chopped

4 orange cheeks, to serve
coriander leaves, to garnish
thinly sliced red chilli, to garnish

continued next page ➤

JERK CHICKEN

WITH COCONUT RICE AND PINEAPPLE SALSA
(continued)

1. Preheat the oven to 170°C.
2. To make the marinade, place all the ingredients in a food processor and process until smooth.
3. Heat a little oil in a large frying pan over high heat. Add the chicken and cook for 4–5 minutes, or until browned all over. Cool, and then place in a roasting pan. Add the marinade, rubbing well into chicken.
4. Cover the pan with foil and roast for 40–45 minutes. Transfer the chicken, skin-side up, to an oven tray. Strain the marinade and juices into a saucepan.
5. Place the chicken under a hot grill and cook until golden and crisp. Simmer the marinade until thickened.
6. To make the coconut rice, heat the oil in a large saucepan over medium heat. Add the onion, chilli and garlic and cook for 3–5 minutes, or until soft. Stir in the rice, then the coconut milk, water and stock. Bring to the boil, then reduce the heat and simmer, covered, for 25 minutes. Remove from the heat and stand, covered, for 10 minutes. Using a fork, fluff the rice and season with salt and pepper. Stir through the beans.
7. To make the pineapple salsa, combine all ingredients in a small bowl.
8. To make the yoghurt salsa, combine all ingredients in a small bowl
9. Divide the chicken among 4 plates and drizzle with the reduced marinade. Serve with rice, salsa, yoghurt and 1 orange cheek on the side and garnish with coriander leaves and red chilli.

This marinade would work well with pork and the yoghurt sauce and pineapple salsa would also be great served with an Indian curry.

'Broken' rice is rice that has not stayed intact during the milling process. If you cannot find it at your local Asian grocer, you can make your own by pulsing the rice in a food processor a few times. Glutinous rice, also known as sticky rice, is available at specialty Asian supermarkets.

CRAB CONGEE

PREP 1 HOUR   COOK 1 HOUR 30 MINS   SERVES 4

2 green mud crabs (1.6kg)
50g glutinous rice
50g broken jasmine rice

CONSOMMÉ

2 litres water
600g chicken carcasses
400g chicken legs, bone-in, skinless
100ml sake
25g ginger, peeled and chopped
1 spring onion, trimmed and chopped
½ bulb garlic, cloves peeled and chopped
½ daikon, chopped
1 tsp white peppercorns
1 small piece kombu
1 tsp oyster sauce
2 stalks Chinese celery, chopped
salt and pepper, to taste

GARLIC GINGER OIL

60ml peanut oil
¼ tsp sesame oil
25g grated ginger
1 clove garlic, peeled and crushed

micro herbs and thinly sliced spring onion, to garnish

1 To make the consommé, bring all the ingredients except the celery to a simmer. Simmer gently, uncovered, for 1½ hours, skimming the surface of any scum throughout. Add the celery for the last 2 minutes of cooking. Strain and discard the solids and season to taste.

2 To make the garlic ginger oil, place all the ingredients in a cold pan. Cook over low heat until the garlic and ginger brown lightly. Remove from the heat and strain and reserve the oil.

3 To prepare the crabs, remove the claws from the body. Cook the claws in boiling salted water for 10 minutes. Remove and place in iced water for 5 minutes. Drain.

4 Add the crab bodies to the same pan. Return to the boil and boil for 15 minutes. Remove and place in iced water for 5 minutes. Drain.

5 Remove the meat from the claws and body in as large pieces as possible.

6 Process the glutinous rice in a small processor until broken.

7 Rinse both rices until the water runs clear. Place in a medium-sized saucepan and cover with 1 litre of cold water. Season to taste and bring to the boil. Simmer gently, partially covered, stirring often, for about 45 minutes, or until soft, thick and porridge-like.

8 Divide the rice among 4 dishes. Top with the crab meat and pour over the consommé. Garnish with herbs and onions. Drizzle with garlic ginger oil.

PASTA WITH CHORIZO AND PESTO

PREP 50 MINS + RESTING TIME   COOK 12–15 MINS   SERVES 4

500g heirloom cherry tomatoes, halved
150g pitted Kalamata olives, halved
1 yellow capsicum, deseeded and diced
1 long red chilli, thinly sliced
1 clove garlic, peeled and crushed
1 cup basil leaves, torn
2 tbsp marjoram leaves
1 tbsp red wine vinegar
1 tbsp olive oil
1 chorizo, skin removed, thinly sliced

PESTO

1 bunch basil
40g pine nuts
2 cloves garlic, peeled
50g finely grated Parmesan
125ml olive oil
1 tbsp lemon juice
salt and pepper, to taste

PASTA

400g Italian '00' flour, plus extra, to dust
1 tsp salt
4 whole eggs
1 tbsp extra-virgin olive oil
1 tbsp water

FLAT BREAD

220g plain flour, plus extra, to dust
½ tsp salt
150ml milk
30g butter, melted
1 tbsp olive oil
1 clove garlic, peeled, crushed
1 tsp finely chopped fresh oregano

1 To make the pesto, place the basil, nuts, garlic and Parmesan in a food processor and process until smooth. With the motor still running, slowly drizzle in the oil, then the lemon juice, and process until combined. Season with salt and pepper, then refrigerate until required.

2 To make the pasta, place the flour and salt on a work surface. Make a well in the centre and crack the eggs into it. Using a fork, whisk the eggs and gradually bring in the flour from the sides. Continue stirring and kneading until well combined. Transfer to a clean, lightly floured surface and knead for 10 minutes, or until dough is smooth and elastic. Wrap in cling film and set aside for 30 minutes.

3 Divide the dough into 8 equal-sized portions and keep covered. Using a rolling pin, flatten 1 portion until 5mm thick and about 12cm wide – nearly the width of your pasta machine.

4 Set the pasta machine to its widest setting, then feed the dough through, narrowing the settings one notch at a time until you reach the thinnest setting and have a 1mm-thick sheet. Pass through a linguine attachment and toss with flour to coat. Repeat with the remaining dough.

5 To make the bread, combine the flour and salt in a bowl. Make a well in the centre and pour in the combined milk, butter, oil, garlic and oregano. Using a fork, stir until combined. Turn out onto a lightly floured surface and knead for 5 minutes, or until smooth and elastic. Cover the dough in cling film and set aside for 30 minutes. Divide the dough into 4 equal-sized portions and roll each portion into a thin round.

6 Combine the tomatoes, olives, capsicum, chilli, garlic, herbs, vinegar and oil in a large bowl. Season with salt and pepper. Preheat a frying pan over high heat, then add the chorizo and cook for 5 minutes, or until crisp. Add the tomato mixture and gently toss to combine and warm through.

7 Cook the bread rounds, one at a time, in a lightly oiled frying pan over medium heat until crisp and golden on both sides. Cut into wedges.

8 Cook the pasta in a large saucepan of salted boiling water for 4–6 minutes, or until just tender. Drain, then add to the bowl with the tomato mixture. Toss to combine. Divide the pasta among 4 bowls, top with pesto and serve with the bread.

If time allows, marinate the steaks overnight, which will give a good depth of flavour.

BAHARAT BEEF
WITH SWEET POTATO MASH AND MINT YOGHURT SAUCE

PREP 1 HOUR + MARINATING COOK 1 HOUR SERVES 4

4 x 150g scotch fillet steaks, at room temperature
1 tbsp olive oil

ROAST TOMATOES

500g cherry vine tomatoes
2 tsp olive oil

SPICE MARINADE

2 tbsp olive oil
1 tbsp sweet paprika
3 tsp ground black pepper
3 tsp ground cumin
2 tsp ground coriander
2 tsp ground cinnamon
1 tsp ground cloves
1 tsp ground cardamom
½ tsp ground star anise
¼ tsp ground nutmeg

MINT YOGHURT SAUCE

250g plain yoghurt
juice of 1 lime
1 garlic clove, peeled
1 cup fresh mint leaves
a pinch of cayenne pepper
a pinch of ground cumin
a pinch of sweet paprika

SWEET POTATO MASH

1kg sweet potatoes, peeled and thickly sliced
salt and pepper, to taste
1 lime
¼ cup finely chopped coriander
2 tbsp mango chutney
1 tbsp soy sauce
1 tbsp butter
1 long red chilli, finely chopped

1 To make the spice marinade, combine all ingredients in a large bowl. Add the beef and rub in the marinade. Refrigerate, covered, for several hours or overnight.

2 To make the mint yoghurt sauce, process all ingredients until smooth.

3 To make the mash, preheat the oven to 200°C. Place the potatoes in a deep baking dish and season to taste. Zest the lime and set aside the zest. Cut the lime in half and place, cut side down, on top of the potatoes. Cover the dish tightly with foil and roast for 30 minutes, or until very tender. Remove the foil, being careful of escaping steam. Squeeze the cooked limes over the potatoes. Mash the potatoes, add the reserved lime zest and the remaining ingredients, then mash again to combine.

4 Place the tomatoes on an oven tray. Drizzle with oil and season to taste. Roast for 15–20 minutes, or until tender, charred and split.

5 Season the steaks with salt. Heat half the oil in a large frying pan over medium–high heat. Cook 2 of the steaks for 2–3 minutes on each side. Transfer to a warm plate and stand for 5 minutes. Wipe the pan clean. Repeat with the remaining steaks.

6 Serve the sliced beef with mash, tomatoes and sauce.

NASI GORENG

PREP 25 MINS + 30 MINS REFRIGERATION   COOK 45 MINS   SERVES 4

4 chicken drumsticks

MARINADE

125ml soy sauce
2–3 tbsp caster sugar
2cm piece ginger, grated
1 clove garlic, peeled and crushed
1 long red chilli, deseeded and finely chopped
1 tsp shrimp paste

NASI GORENG

2 cups white long-grain rice, washed
2 tbsp vegetable oil
1 onion, peeled and diced
1 carrot, diced
1 clove garlic, peeled and finely chopped
1cm piece ginger, peeled and grated
1 long red chilli, deseeded and finely chopped
1 bunch baby bok choy, trimmed and thinly sliced
2 tbsp soy sauce
1 tbsp brown sugar
salt and pepper, to taste

4 fried eggs, to serve
sliced spring onion, to garnish
sliced red chilli, to garnish

1 Preheat the oven to 180°C. To make the marinade, place all the ingredients in a food processor and process until combined. Place in a medium bowl with the chicken and stir to coat. Cover and refrigerate for 30 minutes.

2 Transfer the chicken and marinade to a greased baking tray and roast, turning halfway through, for 35 minutes, or until cooked through.

3 To make the *nasi goreng*, bring 750ml water to the boil in a large saucepan. Add the rice and return to the boil. Reduce the heat to low and simmer, covered, for 15 minutes. Remove from the heat and set aside for 15 minutes. Using a fork, fluff the rice.

4 Preheat the oil in a wok over high heat. Add the onion and carrot and stir-fry until almost tender. Add the garlic, ginger and chilli and stir-fry for 1 minute. Stir in the rice to combine, then add the bok choy and stir until tender. Combine the soy sauce and sugar, stir through the rice and season with salt and pepper.

5 Divide the *nasi goreng* and chicken among 4 plates. Top with 1 fried egg and garnish with onion and chilli to serve.

SEASON 4 · DAN & STEPH

SEASON 4 · ASHLEE & SOPHIA

HAINAN CHICKEN
WITH THREE SAUCES

PREP 40 MINS COOK 1 HOUR SERVES 4

1½ kg whole free-range chicken, at room temperature
1 tbsp sesame oil
2½ cups jasmine rice
3 cups water

NUOC CHAM

60ml warm water
1 tbsp raw sugar
2 bird's-eye chillies, deseeded and finely chopped
1 clove garlic, peeled and finely chopped
60ml fish sauce
2 tbsp rice wine vinegar
2 tbsp fresh lime juice

GINGER SPRING ONION OIL

80ml peanut oil
2 tbsp grated ginger
4 spring onions, trimmed and finely chopped
¾ tsp salt

FRESH CHILLI SAUCE

1 tbsp white vinegar
1 tbsp raw sugar
½ tsp salt flakes
4 bird's-eye chillies, finely diced
4 cloves garlic, peeled and finely diced
2 tbsp grated ginger

POACHING LIQUID

3½ litres water
250ml Shaoxing wine
½ bunch spring onions, green part only, trimmed cut into 6cm lengths
7 thick slices fresh ginger, unpeeled
5 cloves garlic, peeled
½ tsp salt
1 tbsp light soy sauce

finely chopped coriander leaves, thinly sliced long red chilli and spring onions, to garnish

1. To make the *nuoc cham*, stir the water and sugar in a small bowl until the sugar has dissolved. Stir in the remaining ingredients.
2. To make the ginger spring onion oil, heat the oil in a small saucepan over medium heat until hot. Add the ginger, spring onions and salt then stir continuously for 30 seconds. Remove from heat and set aside.
3. To make the fresh chilli sauce, stir the vinegar, sugar and salt in a small bowl until sugar dissolves. Stir in the chillies, garlic and ginger.
4. To cook the chicken, bring all the ingredients for the poaching liquid to the boil in a large stockpot. Add the chicken, breast-side down, and return to the boil. Reduce the heat to low and simmer, covered, for 25 minutes. Turn off the heat and allow to stand, covered, for 30 minutes.
5. Remove the chicken and pat dry with paper towel. Brush the chicken with sesame oil and wrap in cling film. When ready to serve, joint the chicken by cutting away the thighs, drumsticks and wings. Remove the breasts and slice thickly.
6. Meanwhile, place the rice in a medium bowl and cover with water. Stir to rinse out the starch, then drain. Repeat three times until the water stays clear.
7. Place rice and water in a large saucepan and bring to the boil. Reduce the heat and simmer, covered, fluffing with a fork halfway through, for 10 minutes. Fluff again and stand, covered, until ready to serve.
8. Garnish the chicken with coriander, chilli and spring onions. Serve with the rice and sauces.

POACHED PORK BELLY
WITH GREEN BEANS AND BRANDY SAUCE

PREP 40 MINS COOK 3 HOURS SERVES 4

1.2kg piece boneless pork belly
salt, to rub
1 tbsp olive oil
300g green beans
2 tsp lemon juice
a pinch of dried oregano

POACHING LIQUID

750ml chicken stock
750ml full-cream milk
4 bay leaves
1 bunch thyme
1 clove garlic, bruised

PUMPKIN PURÉE

600g pumpkin, peeled and chopped
1 clove garlic
1 tbsp olive oil
salt and pepper, to taste
60ml double cream
2 tbsp butter

BRANDY SAUCE

1 tbsp olive oil
1kg chicken wings
1 onion, peeled and chopped
1 carrot, chopped
200ml brandy
1 litre salt-reduced chicken stock
1 bouquet garni

1 Preheat the oven to 170°C. Cut the skin away from the pork. Score the skin lightly in a criss-cross pattern. Rub all over with salt and half the oil. Refrigerate, uncovered, until required.

2 Cut the pork into 4 portions and place in a deep roasting dish, just big enough to fit.

3 Bring all the poaching liquid ingredients to the boil in a large saucepan. Pour over the pork in the dish and cover tightly with foil. Poach in the oven for 2½–3 hours, or until very tender.

4 To make the pumpkin purée, place the pumpkin and garlic on an oven tray, drizzle with the oil and season to taste. Roast for 30–40 minutes, or until very tender then remove from oven. Squeeze the garlic out of its skin. Process the garlic, pumpkin and remaining ingredients in a food processor until smooth, and season to taste.

5 Increase the oven temperature to 200°C. Place the pork skin on a baking tray and roast for 30–40 minutes, or until golden and crisp.

6 Cook the beans in a saucepan of boiling salted water until tender. Drain and toss with the remaining oil, lemon juice and oregano. Season to taste.

7 To make the brandy sauce, heat the oil in a deep frying pan over medium heat. Cook the chicken wings, onion and carrot, stirring occasionally, for 10 minutes, or until browned. Add the brandy to deglaze the pan.

8 Simmer for 20 minutes, or until reduced by half, then add the stock and bouquet garni. Season with pepper to taste. Simmer until thickened and reduced to about 500ml. Strain and discard the solids.

9 Remove the pork belly from the oven and serve with the beans, crackling and sauce.

Using a deep dish just big enough to fit the pork will ensure it is fully submerged in the poaching liquid and does not dry out during cooking.

If time allows, prepare the roulade a day in advance up to the end of Step 5. This will ensure you have adequate time for it to set. The natural gelatine and fat in the lamb is what holds the roulade together.

LAMB ROULADE

WITH BARLEY, SMOKED CARROTS AND MINT PESTO

PREP 2 HOURS + REFRIGERATION TIME   COOK 5 HOURS   SERVES 6

600g pearl barley
6 baby carrots, peeled
6 baby turnips, trimmed
2 tbsp olive oil
40g butter, cubed
1 cup hickory woodchips, soaked in water for 1 hour
6 finger fennel bulbs, steamed

LAMB STOCK

1½ kg lamb bones
2 onions, peeled and cut into wedges
2 celery stalks, chopped
2 carrots, chopped
2 bay leaves
4 flat-leaf parsley sprigs
2 thyme sprigs
1 rosemary sprig
2 tomatoes, chopped
3 cloves garlic, unpeeled
8 peppercorns
2 tbsp olive oil
5 litres water
salt and pepper, to taste

LAMB ROULADE

2kg lamb shoulder, bone intact
1 litre salt-reduced chicken stock
6 cloves garlic, peeled and crushed
4 rosemary sprigs, leaves removed
5 lemons, halved
1 tbsp olive oil

MINT PESTO

1 bunch mint leaves
½ bunch parsley leaves
1 eschalot, peeled and chopped
2 cloves garlic, peeled
zest of 1 lemon
75g cashews
60g grated Parmesan
125ml extra-virgin olive oil

1 To make the lamb stock, preheat the oven to 200°C. Place the lamb bones, onions, celery and carrots in a large roasting pan and roast for 1 hour. Transfer the bone mixture to a large stockpot with the remaining ingredients and season to taste. Bring to the boil, then reduce the heat to low and simmer, uncovered, for 3 hours, or until aromatic and reduced to about 2 litres. Strain into a large bowl, discarding the solids. Season to taste.

2 Meanwhile, to make the lamb roulade, reduce the oven temperature to 150°C. Place the lamb shoulder in a large roasting pan, then add the chicken stock, garlic, rosemary and lemons. Cover with foil and roast for 3 hours.

3 To make the mint pesto, process all the ingredients except the oil, until finely chopped. Gradually add the oil, processing until combined. Season to taste. Refrigerate until required.

4 Remove the lamb from the oven. Remove the meat from the cooking liquid and shred coarsely into a large bowl. Add 2 tablespoons of the liquid, including the rosemary, to the bowl and season to taste. Form the lamb into an 8cm-diameter roll on a sheet of cling film. Wrap tightly, twisting the ends to form a sausage shape. Refrigerate for 2 hours, or until firm.

5 Meanwhile, place the barley in a large bowl and cover with 500ml water. Set aside for 30 minutes, then strain and transfer to a large stockpot with 1½ litres of the lamb stock. Bring to the boil over high heat, then reduce the heat to low and simmer, partially covered, stirring often, for 40 minutes, or until cooked through and most of the stock has been absorbed.

6 Return the oven heat to 150°C . Place the carrots and turnips on an oven tray, drizzle with the oil and season to taste. Roast for 45 minutes, or until tender.

continued next page ➤

LAMB ROULADE

WITH BARLEY, SMOKED CARROTS AND MINT PESTO

(continued)

7 To make the lamb jus, place the remaining lamb stock in a medium-sized saucepan over medium–high heat and simmer for 8–10 minutes, or until reduced by half. Bring to the boil, then add the butter and whisk to combine.

8 Line a wok or large saucepan with foil, then spread the woodchips on top. Light the woodchips with a blow torch and place over medium heat. Allow to smoke, covered, for 2 minutes. Remove the lid and add the carrots on a rack to sit above the woodchips. Smoke, covered, for 4 minutes.

9 Increase the oven temperature to 180°C. Remove the cling film from the lamb and slice into 6 even pieces. Heat the oil in a large non-stick frying pan over medium heat. Add the lamb and cook for 1–2 minutes on each side, or until golden brown. Transfer to an oven tray and bake for 8 minutes.

10 Divide the barley and vegetables among 6 plates. Add the lamb, top with the pesto and drizzle with jus.

HAPUKU WITH BLACK OLIVE SAUCE
VEGGIE CHIPS AND ROASTED TOMATOES

PREP 20 MINS   COOK 30 MINS   SERVES 4

4 x 150g skinless hapuku fillets
juice of 1 lemon
salt and pepper, to taste
80ml olive oil
25g butter, sliced into 4 pieces
2 tbsp finely chopped parsley
16 vine-ripened cherry tomatoes

VEGGIE CHIPS

vegetable oil, for deep-frying
250g sweet potato, peeled and thinly sliced
200g parsnip, peeled and thinly sliced
240g beetroot, peeled and thinly sliced

BLACK OLIVE SAUCE

1½ cups seedless Kalamata olives
1 long red chilli, deseeded and finely chopped
½ cup coarsely chopped parsley
1 yellow capsicum, deseeded and finely chopped
1 clove garlic, peeled and finely chopped
juice of 1 lemon
60ml extra-virgin olive oil
1 tbsp balsamic vinegar

lemon wedges, to serve

1 Preheat the oven to 200°C. Cut out 4 sheets of baking paper, large enough to wrap each fish fillet.

2 Drizzle the fish with lemon, then season well with salt and pepper.

3 Heat 20ml of oil in a large non-stick frying pan over high heat. Add the fish and cook for 1–2 minutes on each side, or until lightly browned. Place 1 fillet of fish in the centre of each piece of baking paper. Top with 1 butter slice each. Sprinkle over the parsley and drizzle with 20ml of oil. Fold and twist the baking paper to form a parcel.

4 Place on an oven tray and cook in the oven for 5–10 minutes, or until the fish is just cooked through.

5 Place the tomatoes in a roasting dish. Drizzle with the remaining oil, then season to taste. Roast for 8–10 minutes, or until tender.

6 To make the veggie chips, fill a deep-fryer or large saucepan one-third full with vegetable oil and heat over medium heat to 180°C (or until a cube of bread turns golden in 10 seconds). Working in batches of each vegetable, gently drop into the oil and fry, turning halfway, for 2–5 minutes, depending on the cooking time of each vegetable, or until crisp and golden. Remove with a slotted spoon and drain on paper towel. Sprinkle with salt.

7 To make the sauce, process all ingredients in a food processor until a chunky sauce forms. Season with pepper.

8 Remove the fish fillets from the baking paper and divide among 4 plates. Spoon a little sauce on top. Add the tomatoes, a lemon wedge and veggie chips and serve with the remaining sauce on the side.

You could use any type of firm white fish in this recipe. The exact cooking time will depend on the thickness of the fillets.

SEASON 5 · BREE & JESSICA

PAN-SEARED SWORDFISH
WITH GREEN CURRY AND VIETNAMESE SALAD

PREP 30 MINS COOK 1 HOUR SERVES 4

2 tbsp vegetable oil
2 x 270ml cans coconut milk
500ml fish stock
4 x 200g swordfish fillets, skin removed, trimmed
salt and pepper, to taste

GREEN CURRY PASTE

1 tbsp vegetable oil
3 cloves garlic, peeled and crushed
1 eschalot, peeled and chopped
1 stalk lemongrass, white part only, bruised and roughly chopped
5 long green chillies, seeded and roughly chopped
3cm piece ginger, peeled and chopped
3cm piece galangal, peeled and chopped
3 tbsp dried shrimp
½ tsp lime zest
1 tbsp lime juice
1 cup firmly packed coriander leaves
1 cup firmly packed mint leaves
1 cup firmly packed basil leaves
2 tbsp palm sugar
80ml fish sauce
1 tsp ground cumin
1 tsp ground coriander
1 tsp ground turmeric

SALAD DRESSING

juice of 2 limes
1 tsp rice wine vinegar
3 tsp fish sauce
2 tbsp grated palm sugar
1 long red chilli, seeded and finely chopped
1 clove garlic, peeled and finely chopped

VIETNAMESE SALAD

½ cup finely shredded wombok (Chinese cabbage)
2 radishes, thinly sliced
½ cup bean sprouts
½ cup mint leaves
½ cup coriander leaves

steamed jasmine rice, to serve

1. To make the green curry paste, process all the ingredients in a food processor until a smooth paste forms.
2. Heat half the oil in a large saucepan over medium heat. Add the curry paste and cook, stirring, for 5 minutes, or until fragrant. Add the coconut milk and stock. Bring to the boil, then simmer, uncovered, for 45 minutes, or until thickened.
3. To make the salad dressing, whisk all the ingredients in a large bowl until the sugar has dissolved.
4. Heat a heavy non-stick frying pan over high heat. Brush the fish all over with the remaining oil and season with salt and pepper. Add the fish to the pan and cook for 2 minutes on each side, or until just cooked. Transfer to a warm plate for 3 minutes to rest.
5. Add the salad ingredients to the salad dressing and toss to combine.
6. Top the fish with a little salad and serve with the green curry sauce and the rice and salad on the side.

JAPANESE-INSPIRED POACHED CHICKEN IN A MUSHROOM BROTH

PREP 20 MINS COOK 45 MINS SERVES 4

4 chicken breasts, skin-on
salt, to taste
200g enoki mushrooms
2 spring onions, trimmed and thinly sliced
1 cup coriander leaves

MUSHROOM BROTH

2 tsp peanut oil
100g shiitake mushrooms
150g oyster mushrooms
1 red chilli, finely chopped
1cm piece ginger, peeled and grated
1 clove garlic, peeled and crushed
125ml sake
3 Sichuan peppercorns, bruised
2 star anise
1 cinnamon stick
2 tbsp mirin
2 tbsp soy sauce
1 tbsp white miso paste

1 To make the broth, heat the oil in a large non-stick saucepan over medium heat. Add the mushrooms, chilli, ginger and garlic and cook for 5 minutes, or until softened. Add the sake and simmer for 3 minutes, or until almost evaporated. Stir in the remaining ingredients with 2 litres of water and simmer for 25 minutes, or until reduced by half.

2 Meanwhile, preheat oven to 200°C and line an oven tray with baking paper.

3 Remove the skin from chicken and pat dry. Cut the skin into small pieces and place on prepared the tray. Top with baking paper and place a second oven tray on top to sandwich. Roast for 10 minutes. Remove the top tray and baking paper layer and roast the skin for a further 5 minutes, or until crisp and golden. Transfer the crisp skin to a plate and season with salt.

4 Once the broth has reduced, add the chicken breasts and simmer for 5 minutes. Remove from the heat and stand, covered, for 10 minutes, or until cooked through. Remove the chicken from the broth and place in a bowl. Cover with cling film.

5 Strain the broth through a fine sieve into a large saucepan, discarding the solids. Add the enoki mushrooms and simmer until reduced to 750ml.

6 Divide the broth among 4 bowls, then add the spring onions and coriander. Thickly slice the chicken and place in the centre of each bowl. Top with the crisp skin to serve.

Make this dish more substantial by adding some other vegetables – shredded carrots and sugar snap peas would work well.

Moussaka can be prepared and assembled up to two days in advance. Simply reheat to serve.

BAKED MOUSSAKA
WITH GREEK SALAD

PREP 30 MINS COOK 1 HOUR SERVES 4

- 2 tsp olive oil
- 400g lamb mince
- 1 red onion, peeled and finely chopped
- 2 cloves garlic, peeled and crushed
- 2 tsp ground cinnamon
- 2 tsp dried oregano
- 500g truss tomatoes, finely chopped
- ¼ cup chopped basil leaves
- 2 tbsp chopped oregano leaves
- 2 tbsp chopped parsley leaves
- 1 large eggplant, thinly sliced
- 600g potatoes, peeled and thinly sliced
- olive oil cooking spray
- 40g feta, crumbled

CHEESE SAUCE

- 350ml full-cream milk
- 90g unsalted butter
- 50g plain flour
- 2 egg yolks
- 25g grated Parmesan
- salt and pepper, to taste

SALAD

- 20ml olive oil
- 40ml lemon juice
- ½ tsp dried oregano
- 2 Lebanese cucumbers, thinly sliced
- 2 tomatoes, chopped
- ½ small red onion, peeled and thinly sliced
- 75g seeded Kalamata olives, halved
- 50g feta, crumbled
- 2 tbsp chopped oregano leaves

1. Heat the oil in a large saucepan over medium heat. Add the lamb mince and cook, stirring with a wooden spoon to break up any lumps, until browned all over. Remove from the pan and set aside.
2. Add the onion and garlic to the same pan and cook, stirring, for 5 minutes, or until softened. Return the lamb mince to the pan with the cinnamon and dried oregano. Stir to combine, then stir in the tomatoes. Bring to a simmer, then simmer for 5 minutes, or until thickened. Stir in the herbs.
3. Heat a large frying pan over medium heat. Lightly spray the eggplant and potato with olive oil. Add to the pan and cook for 3 minutes on each side, or until tender and lightly browned.
4. To make the cheese sauce, heat the milk and butter in a medium-sized saucepan for 4 minutes, or until hot. While whisking continuously, gradually add the flour until combined, then whisk for 1 minute, or until thickened and mixture bubbles. Remove from the heat and set aside for 10 minutes to cool slightly. Whisk in the egg yolks and Parmesan, then season to taste.
5. Preheat the oven to 180°C. Divide half the mince mixture over the bases of 4 x 1½ -cup capacity ovenproof dishes. Layer with eggplant, potato, the remaining mince mixture and then finish with a layer of cheese sauce. Sprinkle feta on top. Bake for 30 minutes, or until browned.
6. To make the salad, whisk the oil, lemon juice and dried oregano in a large bowl until combined. Season, then add the remaining ingredients and toss to combine.
7. Serve the moussaka with salad on the side.

SPICED KANGAROO
WITH GARAM MASALA POTATOES AND KACHUMBER SALAD

PREP 25 MINS + 4 HOURS MARINATING COOK 50 MINS SERVES 4

600g kangaroo fillets

SPICE RUB

1 tbsp brown sugar
1 tbsp garam masala
1 tbsp ground cumin
2 tsp ground coriander
2 tsp ground turmeric
2 tsp salt
2 tsp ground cardamom
1 tsp ground cinnamon
1 tbsp vegetable oil

SPICED MANGO CHUTNEY

220g caster sugar
125ml white vinegar
3 mangoes, chopped
1 small onion, peeled and finely chopped
1 bird's-eye chilli, finely chopped
60g candied ginger, finely chopped
60g sultanas
1 clove garlic, peeled and crushed
1 tsp yellow mustard seeds

GARAM MASALA POTATOES

6–8 Kipfler potatoes, peeled and cut into 2cm slices
2 tbsp olive oil
1 tsp cumin seeds, bruised
½ tsp ground turmeric
½ tsp garam masala
a pinch of salt

KACHUMBER SALAD

1 tbsp olive oil
1 tbsp lemon juice
1 small red onion, peeled and chopped
2 tomatoes, chopped
1 Lebanese cucumber, peeled, deseeded and chopped
½ bunch coriander, leaves only
1 large red chilli, deseeded and chopped
50g watermelon, deseeded and chopped
salt and pepper, to taste

1. To make the spice rub, dry-fry the sugar and spices in a small frying pan over low heat for 2 minutes, or until fragrant. Place in a large bowl and stir in the oil. Add the kangaroo and rub to coat. Cover and refrigerate for 4 hours or overnight to marinate.
2. To make the chutney, stir the sugar and vinegar in a medium-sized saucepan over medium heat until the sugar has dissolved. Bring to the boil, then stir in the remaining ingredients. Bring to the boil again, then simmer, partially covered, for 30 minutes, or until thickened. Cool completely.
3. Place the potatoes in a saucepan of cold water. Bring to the boil, then simmer for 6 minutes, or until almost tender. Drain and allow the steam to evaporate.
4. Heat the oil in a large frying pan over medium heat. Add the cumin seeds and stir for 1 minute. Add the potatoes, the remaining spices and the salt. Cook, stirring occasionally, for 7 minutes, or until crisp and golden.
5. To make the salad, whisk the oil and lemon juice in a large bowl. Add the remaining ingredients and toss to combine. Season to taste.
6. Bring the kangaroo to room temperature. Lightly oil a frying pan and heat over medium–high heat. Add the kangaroo to the pan and cook for 3 minutes on each side. Transfer to a warm plate to rest, then thickly slice.
7. Divide the potatoes among 4 plates and top with the sliced kangaroo. Serve with the salad and chutney on the side.

Kangaroo is a great lean meat that needs to be cooked quickly and is best eaten medium–rare. Exact cooking time will depend on thickness of the fillets.

Freekeh is cracked green wheat and is available at selected health food shops and Middle Eastern food shops. If using unpackaged freekeh, rinse it to remove any chaff or stones.

PAN-SEARED SALMON
WITH ROASTED BEETROOT AND FREEKEH SALAD

PREP 20 MINS   COOK 45 MINS   SERVES 4

4 x 150g salmon fillets
oil, for frying

TAHINI YOGHURT

250g Greek-style yoghurt
100g feta
1 tbsp tahini
juice of 1 lemon
1 tsp ground cumin

FREEKEH SALAD

4 small beetroots, quartered
1 tbsp olive oil
salt and pepper, to taste
1 small red onion, peeled and finely chopped
1 clove garlic, peeled and finely chopped
200g freekeh, washed
160ml chicken stock
seeds of 1 pomegranate
⅓ cup finely chopped coriander
⅓ cup finely chopped flat-leaf parsley
⅓ cup finely chopped mint

SALAD DRESSING

3 tsp ground cumin
3 tsp sumac
100ml olive oil
40ml red wine vinegar
juice of 1 lemon
2 cloves garlic, peeled and crushed
1 long red chilli, thinly sliced

chopped toasted macadamias, to serve

1. To make the tahini yoghurt, process all the ingredients in a food processor until combined. Cover and refrigerate until needed.
2. Preheat the oven to 200°C. To make the salad, drizzle the beetroot with half the oil, then season to taste and individually wrap in foil. Place on an oven tray and roast for 30 minutes, or until tender. Cool, then peel and discard the skins. Coarsely chop the beetroot and set aside.
3. Heat the remaining oil in a medium frying pan over medium–high heat. Add the onion and garlic and cook, stirring, for 3 minutes, or until softened. Add the freekeh, stock and 100ml water. Simmer, covered, for 15 minutes, or until tender and liquid has been absorbed. Spread the mixture out onto an oven tray to cool.
4. Meanwhile, to make the salad dressing, dry-fry the spices in a small frying pan over low heat until fragrant. Place in a medium bowl with the remaining ingredients and whisk to combine. Add the cooled freekeh, chopped beetroot and remaining salad ingredients. Toss to combine, then season to taste.
5. Lightly oil a frying pan and heat over medium–high heat. Add the salmon, skin-side down, to the pan and cook for 4 minutes, or until the skin is crisp. Turn and cook for another minute. Transfer to a warm plate for 3 minutes to rest.
6. Spoon the tahini yoghurt onto the centre of 4 plates. Top with the salad, then a piece of salmon. Sprinkle over chopped macadamias to serve.

SCAMPI RISOTTO

PREP 45 MINS COOK 2 HOURS SERVES 4

1 tbsp olive oil, plus 2 tsp extra
20 scampi, peeled and chopped, reserving shells and heads
salt and pepper, to taste
1 small onion, peeled and finely chopped
1 small carrot, finely chopped
½ celery stalk, finely chopped
½ baby fennel bulb, trimmed and finely chopped
1 clove garlic, peeled and finely chopped
½ tsp coriander seeds
1½ tbsp tomato paste
250ml rice bran oil

STOCK

1 tbsp olive oil
1 baby fennel bulb, trimmed and chopped
1 carrot, chopped
1 onion, peeled and chopped
1 celery stalk, chopped
2 cloves garlic, peeled and chopped
250ml white wine
2 litres fish stock
2 star anise
4 cloves

RISOTTO

1 onion, peeled and finely chopped
1 celery stalk, finely chopped
2 cloves garlic, peeled and finely chopped
330g arborio rice
250ml white wine
50g butter
50g mascarpone
½ bunch basil, finely chopped
½ bunch tarragon, finely chopped

1 Heat the olive oil in a medium-sized saucepan over medium heat. Add 4 reserved scampi heads and cook for 5 minutes, or until the shells turn pink. Add the vegetables and cook, stirring, for 6 minutes, or until lightly browned. Stir in the coriander seeds and tomato paste, then cover with rice bran oil. Reduce the heat to very low and cook, stirring frequently, for 1 hour. Strain the mixture through a fine sieve into a bowl, discarding the solids.

2 Meanwhile, to make the stock, heat the oil in a large saucepan over medium heat. Add the vegetables and reserved scampi shells and 12 scampi heads. Cook, stirring occasionally, for 10 minutes or until the vegetables are lightly browned. Add the wine and cook until reduced by half. Stir in the fish stock and spices, cover with a lid and cook for 1 hour. Strain the mixture through a fine sieve into a bowl, discarding the solids, then return the mixture to the pan over medium heat. Cook for 30 minutes, or until reduced to 1 litre.

3 To make the risotto, heat 2 tablespoons of the scampi oil in a large saucepan over medium heat. Add the onion, celery and garlic, then cook, stirring, for 5 minutes, or until softened. Add the rice and cook, stirring, for 2 minutes, or until coated in oil mixture. Add the wine and cook until almost evaporated. Add the hot scampi stock, ½ cup at a time and stirring constantly between additions, until the stock is absorbed and rice is tender but still *al dente*; this will take about 25 minutes. Remove from the heat and stir in the chopped scampi meat, butter, mascarpone and herbs. Cover and set aside for 5 minutes (residual heat will cook the scampi).

4 Heat the extra olive oil in a small frying pan over high heat. Season the reserved whole scampi meat, then cook for 1 minute on each side, or until just cooked.

5 Divide the risotto among 4 bowls and top with scampi meat. Drizzle with scampi oil and serve.

SEASON 6 · JANE & EMMA

PORK CHEEK

WITH APPLE CIDER JUS, CRACKLING AND POTATO CROQUETTES

PREP 40 MINS + 1 HOUR MARINATING COOK 3 HOURS SERVES 6

6 pork cheeks
500ml apple cider
2 cinnamon sticks
2 tsp apple cider vinegar
120g butter
2 carrots, chopped into 2cm cubes
2 swedes, peeled and chopped into 2cm cubes
2 tsp olive oil
2 tbsp sea salt flakes
20cm x 20cm piece pork rind, scored

MARINADE

2 thyme sprigs, chopped
2 rosemary sprigs, chopped
1 clove garlic, peeled and crushed
½ tsp ground star anise
1 tbsp olive oil
salt and pepper, to taste

BRAISING LIQUID

1 carrot, chopped
1 onion, peeled and chopped
½ fennel bulb, trimmed and thinly sliced
1 tbsp honey
100g ginger, peeled and thinly sliced
100ml white wine
60ml fish sauce
60ml light soy sauce
1 tsp rice wine vinegar
1 litre chicken stock

POTATO CROQUETTES

500g potatoes, peeled
15g butter
15g Parmesan
1 egg yolk
a pinch of ground nutmeg
vegetable oil, for deep-frying
plain flour, to dust
1 egg, beaten
80g panko breadcrumbs

snow pea shoots, to garnish

1 To make the marinade, combine all the ingredients in a large bowl. Season with salt and pepper. Add the pork cheeks and toss to coat. Cover and refrigerate for 1 hour.

2 Preheat the oven to 180°C. Preheat a large, lightly oiled heavy-based casserole dish over medium–high heat. Cook the pork cheeks in batches, turning halfway, for 4–5 minutes or until browned. Remove the pork and set aside.

3 To make the braising liquid, add the carrot, onion and fennel to the same dish. Cook, turning, for 10 minutes or until lightly browned. Stir in the honey, ginger, white wine, fish sauce, soy sauce and rice wine vinegar. Simmer for 5 minutes, or until reduced by half. Add the pork and stir in the stock. Cover tightly and bring to a simmer.

4 Transfer the dish to the oven and cook for 1½ hours, or until the pork is very tender. Drain 400ml of liquid and place in a saucepan. Remove the pork from the braising liquid and coarsely shred the meat.

5 Add the cider, cinnamon and vinegar to the reserved braising liquid and boil gently for 20 minutes, or until reduced by half. Strain the mixture through a fine sieve into a clean saucepan. Simmer for a further 10 minutes, or until reduced by half again. Whisk in 100g of butter, one cube at a time, until combined. Season to taste.

continued next page ➤

PORK CHEEK

WITH APPLE CIDER JUS, CRACKLING AND POTATO CROQUETTES

(continued)

6 Place the carrots and swedes in a saucepan of cold salted water. Bring to the boil, then simmer for 20 minutes, or until tender. Drain and return to pan. Add the remaining butter and season to taste. Using a fork, lightly mash.

7 To make the croquettes, place the potatoes in a saucepan of cold water, bring to the boil and cook for 30 minutes, or until tender. Drain, return to the saucepan and mash over low heat until smooth. Mash in the butter, then season to taste. Transfer to a bowl and cool slightly. Stir in the Parmesan, egg yolk and nutmeg. When cool enough to handle, roll the mixture into 6 walnut-sized balls and set aside.

8 Rub the oil and salt flakes all over the pork rind. Cut into 3cm x 5cm pieces. Place on a baking tray and top with another tray the same size. Place in the oven and roast for 30 minutes, or until very crisp.

9 Fill a deep-fryer or large saucepan one-third full with vegetable oil and heat over medium heat to 180°C (or until a cube of bread turns golden in 10 seconds). Working in batches, dip the croquettes into the flour, then into the beaten egg, allow the excess to drain off, then coat in breadcrumbs. Gently drop the croquettes into the oil and fry, turning halfway, for 2 minutes, or until crisp and golden. Remove with a slotted spoon and drain on paper towel.

10 Divide the pork among 6 plates. Add the carrots and swede mash, croquettes and crackling to each plate. Garnish with snow pea shoots, then spoon over the jus to serve.

SEASON 6 · ANNIE & LLOYD

LAMB RACK
WITH GREEN OLIVE GREMOLATA AND POMMES DAUPHINE

PREP 25 MINS COOK 45 MINS SERVES 4

500g potatoes, peeled
salt and pepper, to taste
2 eggs
40g unsalted butter, diced
75g plain flour
4 x 4-cutlet lamb racks
vegetable oil, for deep-frying

GREMOLATA

½ cup finely chopped parsley
2 tsp finely grated lemon zest
1 clove garlic, peeled and crushed
1 tbsp lemon juice
70g pitted green olives, finely chopped

1. To make the gremolata, combine all the ingredients in a bowl. Set aside until required.
2. Place the potatoes in a saucepan of cold water, bring to the boil and cook for 35 minutes, or until tender. Drain. Pass the potatoes through a ricer, then season to taste. Cool slightly, then stir in one of the eggs.
3. Bring the butter and ½ cup water to the boil in a saucepan. Remove from the heat, add the flour and stir vigorously until a dough forms. Transfer to a bowl and allow to cool slightly. Beat in the remaining egg until the dough is smooth and shiny. Stir in the potato mixture. Shape 2 teaspoons of the mixture into rounds or ovals and repeat with the remaining dough.
4. Preheat the oven to 220°C. Lightly oil a frying pan and heat over medium–high heat. Add the lamb, fat side down, and cook for 5 minutes, or until browned. Transfer to an oven tray and roast for 10 minutes. Remove from the oven and stand, lightly covered with foil, for 10 minutes to rest.
5. Fill a deep-fryer or large saucepan one-third full with vegetable oil and heat over medium heat to 180°C (or until a cube of bread turns golden in 10 seconds). Working in batches, gently drop the *pommes dauphine* into the oil and fry, turning halfway, for 4 minutes, or until crisp and golden. Remove with a slotted spoon and drain on paper towel. Season with salt and pepper.
6. Divide the lamb racks among 4 plates. Serve with *pommes dauphine* and gremolata.

KERALAN FISH MOILEE
WITH LEMON RICE

PREP 30 MINS + 30 MINS MARINATING COOK 40 MINS SERVES 4

4 tsp ground turmeric
salt, to rub
800g firm white fish fillets, cut into 6cm pieces
4 tbsp olive oil
½ onion, peeled and thinly sliced
1 stalk lemongrass, white part only, finely chopped
4 slices galangal
3 long green chillies, seeded and thinly sliced on the diagonal
270ml coconut milk
a pinch of salt
2 tbsp lemon juice

LEMON RICE

4 tbsp ghee
3 tsp yellow mustard seeds
3 tbsp split mung beans
3 tbsp slivered almonds
3 tsp ground ginger
3 dried chillies, broken into pieces
10 curry leaves, chopped
1 tsp asafoetida
a pinch of salt
1 tsp turmeric powder
300g cooked basmati rice, cooled
juice of 2–3 lemons
½ cup roughly chopped coriander

GARNISH

1 tbsp ghee
1 tsp black mustard seeds
1 onion, peeled and thinly sliced
2cm piece ginger, peeled and thinly sliced
2 cloves garlic, peeled and thinly sliced
8 curry leaves

1 Rub 1 teaspoon of turmeric and salt all over fish. Cover and refrigerate for 30 minutes to marinate.

2 Heat 1 tablespoon of olive oil in a large frying pan over high heat. Cook the fish in batches for 2–3 minutes on each side, or until lightly browned. Remove and set aside.

3 Heat the remaining oil in a large wok over medium heat. Add the onion, lemongrass, galangal and remaining turmeric. Cook, stirring, for 3 minutes, or until softened. Add the chilli, coconut milk and salt and stir to combine. Reduce the heat to low–medium and slowly bring to a simmer. Add the fish, then simmer for 8–10 minutes, or until almost cooked through. Remove the pan from the heat and stir in the lemon juice. Allow to stand for 5 minutes.

4 To make the lemon rice, heat the ghee in a wok over medium heat. Add the mustard seeds and fry until the ghee starts to splutter. Add the mung beans and almonds and fry until lightly golden. Add the ginger, chilli, curry leaves, asafoetida, salt and turmeric and stir-fry for 1 minute.

5 Add the rice and stir to combine. Cook for a further 2 minutes to heat through. Remove from the heat, then add the lemon juice and coriander. Stir to combine.

6 To make the garnish, heat the ghee in a small frying pan. Add the mustard seeds and fry until the ghee starts to splutter. Add the onion, ginger and garlic, then fry for 8–10, minutes or until softened. Add the curry leaves and stir to combine.

7 Divide the rice among 4 plates, then spoon over the curry. Sprinkle over the garnish to serve.

SEASON 6 · DRASKO & BIANCA

MEXICAN PORK RIBS
WITH WHITE BEANS AND PICKLED ONIONS

PREP 30 MINS + 1 HOUR MARINATING   COOK 3 HOURS   SERVES 4

2 pork rib racks, halved
500ml beef stock
2 x 400g can cannellini beans, drained

RIB SAUCE

3 dried ancho chillies, deseeded, seeds reserved
3 dried guajillo chillies, deseeded, seeds reserved
220g tomato purée
110g dark brown sugar
125ml sweet sherry
125ml cider vinegar
15 drops Worcestershire sauce
juice of 2 limes
6 cloves garlic, peeled and chopped
1 bunch coriander stalks
1 tbsp dried oregano
3 tsp medium chilli powder
3 tsp cumin seeds, toasted
2 tsp ground black pepper

PICKLED ONIONS

2 red onions, peeled and thinly sliced
juice of 2 oranges
2 tbsp cider vinegar

SALSA VERDE

1 bunch coriander, roughly chopped
½ bunch fresh mint leaves
¼ bunch basil leaves, roughly chopped
3 cloves garlic, peeled
2 jalapeño chillies, chopped
100ml olive oil
80ml rice wine vinegar
zest and juice of 1 lime
salt and pepper, to taste

coriander sprigs and sliced jalapeños, to garnish
lime wedges, to serve

1. To make the rib sauce, dry-fry the chillies in a frying pan over medium heat for 2–3 minutes, or until toasted. Place the chilli seeds in a bowl and cover with the water. Set aside for 15 minutes to soften.
2. Drain the soaked chilli seeds and place them with the toasted chillies, 500ml boiling water and the remaining ingredients in a food processor. Process until smooth. Transfer the sauce to a large saucepan over medium heat and bring to the boil. Simmer for 15–20 minutes, or until thickened. Set aside to cool, then refrigerate for 30 minutes, or until cold.
3. Preheat the oven to 160°C. Place the ribs in a large roasting dish and pour over the stock. Cover tightly with foil. Roast, turning halfway, for 2 hours, or until tender.
4. Remove the foil, then transfer the ribs to an oven tray.
5. To make the pickled onions, place the onions in a large bowl of boiling water. Stand for 30 seconds, then drain.
6. Whisk the orange juice and vinegar in a bowl. Add the onions, then refrigerate for 1 hour to marinate.
7. To make the salsa verde, place the herbs, garlic and chilli in a food processor and process until finely chopped. With the motor running, drizzle in the oil and vinegar until combined. Stir in the lemon zest and juice and season to taste. Transfer to a bowl and stir in the drained cannellini beans.
8. Brush the ribs with the sauce and cook under a hot grill, basting frequently with sauce, for 2–3 minutes on each side, or until bubbling and glazed.
9. Divide the ribs among 4 plates and spoon over the bean mixture and pickled onions. Garnish with coriander and jalapeño slices and serve with lime wedges on the side.

PORK FILLET
WITH ORANGE AND FENNEL SLAW AND POTATO RÖSTI

PREP 40 MINS COOK 50 MINS SERVES 4

800g pork fillet
1 tbsp olive oil
½ bunch coriander stalks, finely chopped
1 tbsp white wine
250ml chicken stock
25g butter, chopped

DRESSING

125ml orange juice
1½ tbsp light soy sauce
60ml light olive oil
2cm piece ginger, peeled and finely grated
2 tsps finely grated orange zest

POTATO RÖSTI

800g medium potatoes, unpeeled
25g butter, melted
vegetable oil, for deep-frying

PEAR PURÉE

25g butter
2 ripe pears, peeled and chopped
¼ tsp ground cinnamon
500ml dry apple cider

SLAW

1 small fennel bulb, finely sliced
1 cup finely shredded red cabbage
1 cup finely shredded white cabbage
1 large carrot, julienned
2 spring onions, trimmed and thinly sliced
¼ cup dill sprigs

1 To make the dressing, whisk all the ingredients in a bowl until combined. Set aside.

2 To make the rösti, place the potatoes in a saucepan of cold water. Bring to the boil and boil gently for 5 minutes. Drain, then cool and peel. Coarsely grate the potatoes into a bowl. Stir in the butter and season to taste. Divide the mixture into 8 portions. Using your hands, squeeze out the excess moisture and shape each portion into a pattie. Place on a tray in a single layer and refrigerate until required.

3 To make the pear purée, melt the butter in a saucepan over medium heat. Add the pears and cook, stirring, for 3–4 minutes, or until lightly golden. Stir in the cinnamon, then stir in the cider. Simmer for 6–8 minutes, or until the pears are very soft. Strain and transfer the pears to a food processor, reserving the cider. Process the pears until a purée forms.

4 To make the slaw, place all the ingredients in a bowl. Pour over the dressing and toss to combine.

5 Preheat the oven to 180°C. Place the pork in a bowl. Add the oil, coriander and wine. Season to taste and toss to coat. Heat a frying pan over medium–high heat. Add the pork and cook for about 2 minutes on each side, or until browned. Transfer to an oven tray and roast for about 12–15 minutes, or until just cooked. Remove from the oven and transfer to a warm plate to rest for 5 minutes. Thickly slice.

6 Add the reserved cider mixture to the frying pan the pork was cooked in. Simmer for 10 minutes, or until reduced by half. Stir in the stock and simmer for 5 minutes, or until slightly thickened. Stir in any juices from the rested pork, then whisk in the butter, one cube at a time, until the sauce is glossy. Strain the mixture through a fine sieve, discarding the solids.

7 Fill a deep-fryer or large saucepan one-third full with vegetable oil and heat over medium heat to 180°C (or until a cube of bread turns golden in 10 seconds). Gently drop the rösti into the oil and fry, turning halfway, for 4 minutes, or until crisp and golden. Remove with a slotted spoon and drain on paper towel.

8 Spoon the pear purée into the centre of each serving plate. Top with slaw, pork and rösti. Spoon over the sauce to serve.

To make deep-fried mint leaves, pat the leaves dry and deep-fry until crisp.

CRISPY BARRAMUNDI
WITH APPLE AND MANGO SALAD

PREP 20 MINS COOK 10 MINS SERVES 4

75g plain flour
1 tbsp ground turmeric
1 tbsp ground cumin
salt and pepper, to taste
200g barramundi fillets, skin intact, cut into 2cm strips
vegetable oil, for deep-frying

NAM JIM DRESSING

1–2 long green chillies
2 cloves garlic, peeled
¼ bunch coriander roots
1 tbsp caster sugar
125ml lime juice
2 tbsp fish sauce

SALAD

1 apple, peeled and julienned
1 mango, peeled, deseeded and cut into small dice
1 long green chilli, julienned
1 long red chilli, julienned
1 cup small mint leaves
1 cup coriander leaves
2 kaffir lime leaves, julienned

thinly sliced red chilli and deep-fried mint leaves, to garnish

1. To make the *nam jim* dressing, place the chillies, garlic and coriander in a food processor and process until finely chopped. Add the remaining ingredients and process until combined.
2. To make the salad, place all ingredients in a bowl.
3. Place the flour and spices in a ziplock bag, then season to taste. Add the fish pieces and toss to coat.
4. Fill a deep-fryer or large saucepan one-third full with vegetable oil and heat over medium heat to 180°C (or until a cube of bread turns golden in 10 seconds). Gently drop the fish into the oil and fry, turning halfway, for 4 minutes, or until crisp and golden. Remove with a slotted spoon and drain on paper towel. Season to taste.
5. Add half the dressing to the salad and toss to combine. Season with salt and pepper.
6. Divide salad among 4 plates and top with the fish. Garnish with chilli and mint leaves. Serve with remaining dressing on the side.

CHINESE BRAISED BEEF RIBS

PREP 25 MINS + 4 HOURS MARINATING COOK 3 HOURS 30 MINS SERVES 4

125ml hoisin sauce
10 cloves garlic, peeled and crushed
white pepper, to taste
1½ kg beef ribs

BRAISING MIXTURE

4 spring onions, trimmed and roughly chopped
2cm piece ginger, peeled and thinly sliced
1 tbsp peanut oil
90ml soy sauce
60ml Shaoxing wine
18 dried red dates
150g roasted unsalted peanuts
3 star anise
1 cinnamon stick
2 wide pieces orange peel
750ml chicken stock
1½ tbsp crushed rock sugar

chopped coriander, to garnish
steamed bok choy, to serve

1. Combine the hoisin sauce and garlic in a large dish and season with white pepper. Add the ribs and rub the sauce all over. Cover and refrigerate for 4 hours or overnight to marinate.
2. Preheat the oven to 160°C. To prepare the ribs, using a mortar and pestle, grind the onion and ginger until roughly crushed. Heat half the oil in a flameproof baking dish. Add the onion mixture and cook over medium heat, stirring, for 5 minutes, or until softened. Transfer to another dish and set aside.
3. Scrape the excess marinade off the ribs, reserving the marinade. Heat the remaining oil in the same baking dish over high heat. Add the ribs in batches and cook for 2 minutes on each side, or until browned all over. Add the remaining braising ingredients with the onion mixture and reserved marinade.
4. Bring to the boil, then cover tightly with a lid and transfer to oven. Cook for 2½–3 hours, or until ribs are very tender. Remove the ribs from dish and set aside.
5. Place the dish over medium heat and simmer the sauce for 20 minutes, or until thickened. Remove from the heat and discard the star anise, orange peel and cinnamon stick.
6. Divide the ribs among 4 plates and pour over the sauce. Garnish with coriander and serve with steamed bok choy on the side.

For a shortcut, you can buy ready-made bisque from delicatessens.

MORETON BAY BUGS
WITH CELERIAC REMOULADE AND SEAFOOD BISQUE

PREP 1 HOUR   COOK 1 HOUR 10 MINS   SERVES 4

4 green Moreton Bay Bugs
juice of ½ lemon

BISQUE

25g butter
2 tsp olive oil
1 onion, peeled and chopped
1 stick celery, chopped
1 baby fennel bulb, trimmed and chopped
1 carrot, chopped
2 cloves garlic, peeled and chopped
1 tsp fennel seeds
1 tsp coriander seeds
500g prawn heads
2 tbsp tomato paste
250ml white wine
1kg tomatoes, finely chopped (or processed)
½ bunch basil, chopped
½ bunch parsley, chopped
125ml thickened cream

MAYONNAISE

2 egg yolks
1 tbsp lemon juice
1 tbsp white wine vinegar
300ml light olive oil
1 tsp wholegrain mustard
salt and pepper, to taste

REMOULADE

250g mayonnaise (as above)
1 small celeriac, peeled and julienned
1 tsp baby capers
4 cornichons, finely chopped
2 tsp finely chopped tarragon
2 tsp finely chopped parsley

1. To make the bisque, heat the butter and oil in a large saucepan over low to medium heat. Cook the onion, celery, fennel, carrot, garlic and seeds for about 20 minutes, or until the vegetables are very soft. Using a rolling pin, crush the prawn heads to extract flavour, then add the prawn heads and tomato paste and cook, stirring, for 5 minutes (add a little water if the mixture begins to catch). Add the wine and simmer for approximately 10 minutes, or until reduced by half.
2. Stir in the tomatoes and herbs. Bring to the boil, then reduce the heat and simmer, covered, for 40 minutes.
3. Strain the mixture into a clean saucepan and discard the solids. Simmer until reduced to about 750ml. Stir in the cream then simmer until thickened slightly.
4. To make the mayonnaise, process the egg yolks, juice and vinegar in a food processor until smooth. With the motor still running, drizzle in the oil until the mayonnaise is thick and smooth. Season to taste.
5. To make the *remoulade*, combine all the ingredients in a bowl and season to taste.
6. Place the bugs upside down on a chopping board. Using a sharp knife, cut the heads off. Using kitchen scissors, cut down either side of the tail and peel the underside of the tail back. Remove the meat and season all over.
7. Lightly oil a frying pan and heat over medium–high heat. Add the bug tails and cook for about 2 minutes on each side, or until the flesh is golden and just cooked through. Drizzle with the lemon juice.
8. Arrange the *remoulade* among 4 serving bowls and top with the bug tails. Pour the bisque around the edges.

TEA-SMOKED DUCK
WITH FENNEL PURÉE AND CRANBERRIES

PREP 40 MINS COOK 50 MINS SERVES 4

4 duck breasts, skin scored

CRANBERRY SAUCE
300g frozen cranberries
110g brown sugar
60ml red wine
2 tbsp sherry vinegar
1 tbsp finely grated orange zest
black pepper, to taste

FENNEL PURÉE
25g butter
1 medium fennel bulb, trimmed and chopped
100ml chicken stock
100ml thickened cream
1 tsp lemon juice

SMOKING MIXTURE
½ cup brown sugar
½ cup jasmine rice
½ cup black tea leaves
peel of 1 orange
4 star anise
1 cinnamon stick, broken

steamed broccolini, to serve
snow pea tendrils, to garnish

1. To make the cranberry sauce, stir all the ingredients in a saucepan over medium heat until the sugar has dissolved. Simmer until the cranberries have broken down and mixture is soft and slightly thickened. Season with black pepper and blend until smooth, then pass through a sieve.
2. To make the purée, heat the butter in a saucepan over medium heat. Cook the fennel for approximately 15 minutes, or until tender. Add the stock and cream and simmer, covered, for 10 minutes, or until the fennel is very soft. Strain and reserve the liquid. Blend the fennel until smooth, then add enough of the reserved cooking liquid to form a soft, silky purée. Blend again. Add the lemon juice and season to taste. Pass through a fine sieve.
3. To smoke the duck, line a bamboo steamer basket with baking paper. Season the duck all over and place in the steamer basket in a single layer. Secure the lid. Line the base of a large wok (the same size as the bamboo steamer) with foil. Add the smoking mixture ingredients and place over high heat until the mixture starts to smoke. Place the steamer over the wok, reduce the heat to low and smoke for 10 minutes. Remove from the heat and allow to stand for 5 minutes.
4. Heat a frying pan over medium heat. Add the duck skin-side down and cook for about 4–5 minutes, or until the skin is golden and crisp. Transfer to a warm plate to rest for 5 minutes. Slice.
5. Serve duck with the purée, broccolini and cranberry sauce and garnish with snow pea tendrils.

The exact cooking time of the duck will depend on its size and thickness. Resting the duck is essential to ensure the juices remain in the meat.

You can flavour the lavosh with anything you like – try chopped fresh herbs, grated citrus zest or your favourite spice.

SEARED LAMB
WITH FETA, BEETROOT AND ROSEMARY HONEY

PREP 1 HOUR COOK 1 HOUR 10 MINS SERVES 4

600g lamb fillet or backstrap
olive oil, for brushing
salt and pepper, to taste
½ cup walnut pieces, toasted

BAKED FETA

250ml olive oil
4 cloves garlic, peeled and sliced
4 sprigs fresh rosemary
200g block feta

ROSEMARY HONEY

½ bunch rosemary
125ml honey

LAVOSH

225g plain flour
1 tsp salt
1 tsp caster sugar
1 tbsp sesame seeds
1 tbsp poppy seeds
125ml warm water
60ml light olive oil
1 tsp white vinegar

ROASTED BEETROOT

4 baby beetroot
1 tbsp olive oil
2 cloves garlic, peeled and crushed
1 tbsp balsamic vinegar

BABY LEAF SALAD

2 tbsp olive oil
2 tbsp lemon juice
200g baby beetroot and spinach leaves

1 To bake the feta, first infuse the olive oil by placing the oil, garlic and rosemary in a small saucepan. Season with pepper. Place over very low heat, stirring occasionally, until hot. Remove from the heat and set aside to infuse for 1 hour.

2 To make the rosemary honey, stir all the ingredients in a small saucepan over very low heat, stirring occasionally, until hot. Season to taste. Remove and set aside to cool. Remove the rosemary.

3 Preheat the oven to 180°C. To make the lavosh, sift the combined flour, salt and sugar into a bowl. Stir in the seeds, then stir in the combined water, oil and vinegar to form a dough.

4 Knead on a lightly floured surface for 1 minute. Roll out the dough until about 2mm thick. Cut into thin triangles and place on an oven tray lined with baking paper. Bake for 10–15 minutes or until golden and crisp. Season to taste.

5 To prepare the roasted beetroot, slice the beetroot and place in a roasting pan in a single layer. Drizzle with oil and season to taste. Roast for 30 minutes then remove from oven. Add the garlic and vinegar and toss to coat. Roast for a further 5–10 minutes, or until tender.

6 Reduce the oven temperature to 160°C. Place the feta in a small baking dish and pour over the infused oil mixture. Season with pepper and lightly cover with foil. Bake for 20 minutes.

7 Brush the lamb all over with oil and season to taste. Heat a frying pan over medium–high heat. Cook for about 3 minutes on each side, or until cooked as desired. Transfer to a warm plate to rest, lightly covered with foil, for 5 minutes. Slice.

8 To prepare the salad, toss all ingredients in a bowl.

9 Divide the salad and roasted beetroot among 4 plates. Top with the feta, lamb and walnuts. Drizzle with rosemary honey and serve with lavosh on the side.

CONFIT SALMON
WITH ROASTED FENNEL AND AVOCADO MOUSSE

PREP 45 MINS COOK 50 MINS SERVES 4

1 litre water
60g salt
4 x 100g skinless salmon fillets, pin-boned
800ml olive oil
1 vanilla bean, split and seeds scraped
1 tsp fennel seeds, toasted

ROASTED FENNEL

2 baby fennel bulbs, trimmed and cut into 5mm slices, reserving the fronds
2 tbsp olive oil
2 tsp lemon juice
salt and pepper, to taste

AVOCADO MOUSSE

1 avocado, peeled and deseeded
1 tbsp crème fraîche
1 tbsp lemon juice

CABBAGE SALAD

2 tsp olive oil
2 tsp lemon juice
1 cup thinly sliced white cabbage
2 tbsp fennel fronds

orange salmon roe, to garnish

1 Create a brine for the confit salmon by combining the water and salt in a shallow glass bowl (just big enough to fit the salmon). Add the salmon in a single layer. Refrigerate for 15 minutes.

2 Preheat the oven to 180°C. To make the roasted fennel, place the fennel slices on an oven tray, drizzle with the oil and lemon juice and season to taste. Roast for 20 minutes, turning halfway through, until tender and lightly caramelised.

3 Reduce the oven temperature to 50°C. Remove the salmon from the brine, rinse in clean water and pat dry. Place the olive oil, vanilla and fennel seeds in an oven dish (just big enough to fit the salmon). Place the dish in the oven and bring the oil mixture to 50°C, using a digital thermometer. Add the salmon in a single layer.

4 Bake for about 20 minutes, or until just cooked. The texture should be soft, silky and melting. Remove the salmon and drain on paper towel.

5 Meanwhile, to make the avocado mousse, blend all the ingredients until smooth. Season to taste and refrigerate until required.

6 To make the cabbage salad, whisk the oil and lemon juice in a bowl. Add the cabbage and fennel fronds. Toss to combine and season to taste.

7 Smear the avocado cream onto serving plates and top with the salmon. Serve with the roasted fennel and salad and garnish with salmon roe.

SEASON 6 · JAC & SHAZ

BEEF CHEEKS
WITH PORT AND CELERIAC PURÉE

PREP 1 HOUR 30 MINS COOK 3 HOURS 30 MINS SERVES 4

2 tbsp olive oil
1kg beef cheeks, trimmed
plain flour, for dusting
1 brown onion, peeled and thinly sliced
2 cloves garlic, peeled and sliced
250ml red wine
150ml port
500ml beef stock
thinly peeled zest and juice of 1 orange
1 bunch rosemary, tied together with butcher's string
2 bay leaves

RED WINE SYRUP

300ml red wine
50g caster sugar

CELERIAC PURÉE

800g celeriac, peeled and cut into 3cm pieces
30ml cream
salt and pepper, to taste

PICKLED VEGETABLES

400ml white wine vinegar
55g caster sugar
1 sprig rosemary
1 tsp peppercorns
4 baby carrots, peeled
4 baby turnips, peeled
2 tsp butter

micro herbs, to garnish

1 Preheat the oven to 160°C. Heat half the oil in a flameproof casserole dish over medium–high heat. Dust the beef cheeks in flour and cook, one at a time, until browned all over. Remove and set aside.

2 Add the remaining oil to the same dish. Cook the onion and garlic, stirring, for several minutes, or until lightly browned. Remove from the pan and set aside. Add the wine and port to the pan to deglaze and simmer until reduced by half. Stir in the stock, orange zest and juice, rosemary and bay leaves, then return the beef, onions and garlic to the dish. Bring to the boil then transfer to the oven and cook, covered, for 3 hours, or until the beef is very tender.

3 Meanwhile, to make the red wine syrup, stir the wine and sugar in a saucepan over medium heat until the sugar has dissolved. Simmer for 10 minutes, or until reduced and thickened to form a syrup. Set aside.

4 To make the celeriac purée, place the celeriac in a large saucepan of cold salted water. Bring to the boil and boil gently for 15 minutes, or until tender. Drain, transfer to a blender and blend until smooth. Add the cream and blend to combine. Season to taste, then pass through a sieve.

5 To pickle the vegetables, stir the vinegar, sugar, rosemary and peppercorns in a saucepan over medium heat until the sugar has dissolved. Add the vegetables and simmer, covered, until just tender but still with a slight bite. Remove the vegetables with a slotted spoon.

6 Melt the butter in a frying pan over medium heat. Add the pickled vegetables and cook, tossing, until glazed. Season to taste.

7 Remove the cooked beef from the dish and, cut into pieces. Set aside and cover to keep warm. Place the dish with the sauce over medium heat and cook for 10 minutes, or until reduced and thickened. Remove the bay leaves, rosemary and orange zest. Stir in the red wine syrup to taste.

8 Serve the beef cheeks with the celeriac purée, pickled vegetables and sauce. Garnish with micro herbs.

CURED KINGFISH
WITH YELLOW CURRY

PREP 30 MINS COOK 25 MINS SERVES 4

2 tbsp red rice
400g skinless kingfish fillet, sashimi grade, pin-boned

YELLOW CURRY PASTE

1 tsp cumin seeds, toasted
1 tsp coriander seeds, toasted
2 tbsp peanut oil
1 long dried red chillies, chopped
1 dried bird's-eye chilli
1 stick lemongrass, bruised and chopped
1 eschalot, peeled and chopped
4 cloves garlic, peeled and chopped
1cm piece fresh ginger, peeled and sliced
1-cm piece galangal, peeled and sliced
2 tsp curry powder
1 tsp ground turmeric
1 tsp shrimp paste

CURRY SAUCE

1 quantity curry paste (as above)
270ml can coconut cream
2 tsp reserved curing mixture

CURING MIXTURE

1 clove garlic, peeled and thinly sliced
½ red onion, peeled and thinly sliced
1cm piece fresh ginger, peeled and thinly sliced
1 long red chilli, thinly sliced
juice of 4 limes

micro herbs, to garnish

1 Heat a small heavy-based frying pan over medium heat. Cook the rice, tossing, until it is browned and smells nutty. Allow to cool. Using a mortar and pestle, pound lightly to crush.

2 To make the curry paste, dry-fry the seeds in a small frying pan until fragrant. Allow to cool, then grind to a powder using a mortar and pestle. Transfer to a small food processor and add the remaining ingredients. Process to form a smooth paste.

3 To make the curry sauce, heat a medium-sized saucepan over medium–low heat. Cook the curry paste, stirring occasionally, for 15 minutes, or until soft and very fragrant. Stir in the coconut cream. Reduce the heat to low and simmer for 10 minutes. Set aside to cool, then push the sauce through a sieve and discard the solids.

4 To make the curing mixture, combine all the ingredients in a jug. Set aside for 10 minutes to infuse. Strain, reserving the juice to cure the fish and the red onion to serve. Discard the remaining solids.

5 Cut the fish into 3mm slices. Place the slices in a shallow dish or tray in a single layer. Pour over the infused lime juice. Set aside for 10 minutes. Strain the fish and add 2 teaspoons of the lime juice to the curry sauce. Discard the remaining lime juice.

6 Brush a line of curry sauce onto 4 plates. Top with the cured fish and reserved red onion. Garnish with toasted red rice and micro herbs.

Freeze any leftover curry sauce and use it to make your next curry.

The exact cooking time of quail will depend on its size. Be vigilant during the second cooking time to ensure the quail does not overcook.

QUAIL
WITH CORN AND JUS

PREP 1 HOUR 10 MINS COOK 1 HOUR SERVES 4

1 corn cob
4 jumbo quails
50g butter, melted

JUS

2 tsp olive oil
1kg chicken wings
1 carrot, chopped
1 stick celery, chopped
1 onion, peeled and chopped
4 cloves garlic, peeled and chopped
3 sprigs thyme
3 sprigs rosemary
2 bay leaves
125ml white wine
1 litre chicken stock
25g butter, cut into cubes

CORN PURÉE

4 corn cobs
1 litre milk
1 fresh bay leaf
25g butter
2 sprigs fresh thyme
125ml thickened cream, warmed
salt and pepper, to taste

POPCORN

1 tbsp vegetable oil
¼ cup popping corn kernels
25g butter, melted

micro herbs, to garnish

1. To make the jus, heat the oil in a large deep frying pan over medium heat. Cook the chicken wings, vegetables and herbs, stirring, for approximately 15 minutes, or until the chicken and vegetables are browned. Remove and set aside. Add the wine to deglaze the pan. Simmer, scraping the base of the pan to remove any sticky residue. Add the stock and simmer for 10 minutes, or until reduced by half.
2. Strain the mixture into a clean pan and discard the solids. Stir the jus over medium heat. Whisk in the butter, a cube at a time, until the jus is smooth and glossy.
3. To make the corn purée, place the corn cobs, milk and bay leaf in a large saucepan. Simmer, covered, over medium heat for 10–15 minutes, or until the corn is very tender. Remove the cobs and reserve the milk. Trim the kernels off the cobs, transfer to a blender and blend to form a purée. Add the cream and blend until smooth. Add enough of the cooking milk to form a soft, silky purée. Season to taste and pass through a fine sieve.
4. To make the popcorn, heat the oil in a large saucepan. Add the popping corn kernels and cook, covered, shaking the pan, until the kernels pop. Pour out onto a tray. Drizzle with butter and season to taste. Once cool, process until finely crushed.
5. For the blackened corn, heat a chargrill pan over high heat. Cook the corn, turning, until charred all over. Trim the kernels from cob.
6. Preheat the oven to 200°C. Place the quails in a roasting pan, brush all over with half the melted butter and season to taste. Roast for 10–15 minutes, or until the skin is crisp and a dark golden colour, basting halfway through. When cool enough to handle, cut the breasts and legs off the birds, discarding the carcasses. Return to the roasting pan, skin-side up, and baste with the remaining melted butter. Roast for a further 2–3 minutes, or until just cooked but still pink in the middle.
7. Serve the quail with the corn purée, chargrilled corn and jus. Garnish with micro herbs and crushed popcorn.

RED MULLET
WITH JERUSALEM ARTICHOKE AND BASIL

PREP 40 MINS COOK 1 HOUR 45 MINS SERVES 4

2 tsp olive oil
1 tbsp butter
12 red mullet fillets, skin-on, pin-boned

BASIL OIL

1 tbsp coriander seeds
1 star anise
½ bunch basil, leaves picked
finely grated zest of ½ lemon
2 tsp lemon juice
250ml light olive oil

ARTICHOKE PURÉE

4 Jerusalem artichokes, peeled and chopped
500ml milk
1 bay leaf
1 tbsp butter

HAY-SMOKED ARTICHOKES

hay, for smoking
4 Jerusalem artichokes, peeled
25g butter

PURPLE CARROTS

4 purple Dutch carrots
1 tbsp olive oil
1 tbsp butter
2 tsp lemon juice

micro herbs, to garnish

1. To make the basil oil, dry-fry the coriander seeds and star anise in a frying pan over medium heat for a couple of minutes, or until fragrant. Allow to cool, then crush to a fine powder using a mortar and pestle. Transfer to a small food processor and add the remaining ingredients. Process to form a purée. Set aside to infuse for 1 hour. Season to taste and press the mixture through a sieve to extract the flavoured oil. Set aside.
2. To make the artichoke purée, place the artichokes, milk and bay leaf in a saucepan over low–medium heat. Season to taste and cook, partially covered, for approximately 15 minutes, or until the artichokes are very soft. Drain and reserve the milk. Discard the bay leaf. Transfer the artichokes to a blender and blend until smooth. Add enough of the reserved milk to form a soft, silky purée. Add the butter, season to taste and blend to combine. Pass through a fine sieve.
3. Preheat the oven to 180°C. To make the smoked artichokes, melt half the butter in a frying pan over low heat. Add the artichokes and cook, turning, for approximately 10 minutes, or until golden brown.
4. Place a cake pan covered with a rack in an oven dish (which has a lid). Cover the base of the pan and the dish with the hay. Sprinkle evenly with a little water. Using a blow torch, set the hay alight in several places, putting out the flames immediately. Re-light, agitating the hay for an even burn and put out again. Re-light a final time, put out and place the artichokes on the rack. Cover with the lid immediately to trap the smoke. Transfer to the oven and roast for 30 minutes, or until the artichokes are tender.

continued next page ➤

Hay should be available at your local nursery or garden centre.

RED MULLET
WITH JERUSALEM ARTICHOKE AND BASIL

(continued)

5 Place the carrots in a small oven dish. Toss with the olive oil and season. Roast for 35 minutes, or until tender, turning halfway through. Remove from the dish, trim the ends and cut in half lengthways.

6 Melt the butter in a frying pan over medium heat. Toss the carrots in the butter to glaze, then stir in the lemon juice. Season to taste.

7 To finish cooking the smoked artichokes, melt the remaining butter in a frying pan over medium–high heat. Cook the artichokes a final time, turning, to crisp on the outside. Season to taste.

8 Pat the fish dry with paper towel and season to taste. Heat the oil and butter in a frying pan over medium heat. Cook the fish skin-side down for 5–6 minutes, or until crisp. Turn and cook for a further 30 seconds to 1 minute, or until the fish is just cooked through.

9 Arrange the fish, purée and smoked artichoke on serving plates. Add the carrots, sprinkle with micro herbs and drizzle with basil oil.

CONFIT DUCK LEG

WITH HONEY-GLAZED BEETROOT AND COMPRESSED WATERMELON

PREP 45 MINS COOK 4 HOURS SERVES 4

4 duck Marylands
500g duck fat

CURING MIXTURE

2 tbsp salt
1 tbsp thyme leaves
1 tbsp rosemary leaves
2 tsp black peppercorns

HONEY-GLAZED BEETROOT

4 baby beetroot, trimmed
2 tsp coriander seeds
2 tsp cumin seeds
125ml sherry vinegar
100g unsalted butter
125ml honey
salt and pepper, to taste
2 tsp lemon juice

BEETROOT REDUCTION

80ml beetroot juice
50ml sherry vinegar
1 tbsp honey

COMPRESSED WATERMELON

15cm square piece seedless watermelon, 2cm thick
2 tsp white wine vinegar

red-veined sorrel leaves, to garnish

1. To make the curing mixture, combine all the ingredients in a large bowl. Add the duck and rub all over. Refrigerate, covered, in a single layer, for 30 minutes or overnight.
2. Preheat the oven to 100°C. To make the confit duck, place the duck fat in a deep oven dish (just big enough for the duck) over medium heat until melted. Brush the curing mixture off the duck and add to the dish in a single layer. The duck should be submerged in the melted fat.
3. Transfer to the oven and cook for 2–3 hours, or until the meat is very tender and nearly falling off the bone. Remove from the oven.
4. Increase the oven temperature to 180°C. Place the beetroot in an oven dish and roast for about 40 minutes, or until tender. Peel and cut into 2cm slices.
5. To make the honey glaze, dry-fry the seeds in a saucepan until fragrant. Add the vinegar and simmer for 5–10 minutes, or until reduced by half. Add the butter and honey and season to taste. Simmer for approximately 5 minutes, or until reduced to form a syrup consistency. Strain and discard the solids. Stir in the lemon juice.
6. Heat a frying pan over medium heat. Add the roasted beetroot pieces and enough of the glaze to evenly coat. Cook for 2–3 minutes, or until glossy and lightly caramelised.
7. To make the beetroot reduction, simmer all the ingredients in a saucepan over medium heat for 8–10 minutes, or until reduced and thickened to a syrup consistency.
8. To prepare the compressed watermelon, place the melon in a sous vide bag and vacuum seal, then remove from the bag and cut into 3cm cubes.
9. Lightly oil a frying pan and heat over high heat. Add the watermelon and drizzle with vinegar. Cook, turning, until heated through. Season to taste.
10. Heat a frying pan over medium heat. Cook the confit duck skin-side down until very crisp and dark golden brown.
11. Serve the duck and roasted beetroot with the watermelon and red-veined sorrel. Drizzle with the beetroot reduction and remaining honey glaze.

MKR
MY KITCHEN RULES

DESSERTS

Cheese soufflés and caramelised fruit are a match made in heaven. Try using apples or even peaches for a fruity change.

TWICE-BAKED GORGONZOLA SOUFFLÉS
WITH CARAMELISED PEAR AND VERMOUTH

PREP 30 MIN COOK 55 MIN SERVES 6

2 Beurre Bosc pears, peeled and cored
1 tbsp caster sugar
50g melted butter

SOUFFLÉS

60g butter
50g plain flour
250ml warm milk
85g Gorgonzola cheese, mashed into pieces
1 tbsp grated Parmesan cheese
½ tbsp finely chopped fresh parsley
5 eggs, separated
salt and ground pepper, to taste
1½ cups thickened cream
½ cup sweet Vermouth

1 Preheat the oven to 180°C. Cut the pears into ½ cm slices. Toss with the sugar and melted butter. Arrange in a single layer on an oven tray lined with baking paper. Cook for 15–20 minutes, or until golden. Remove from oven and cover to keep warm.

2 To prepare the soufflés, lightly butter 6 ovenproof dishes (180ml capacity). Melt the butter in a medium-sized saucepan. Add the flour and cook, stirring, over medium heat, for 1 minute. Gradually stir in the milk. Cook, stirring, until the sauce boils and thickens. Remove from the heat. Stir in the cheeses, parsley and egg yolks and season to taste. Transfer the mixture to a large bowl.

3 Whisk the egg whites until soft peaks form. Fold half the egg whites quickly into the cheese mixture and repeat with the remaining egg whites. Divide the mixture among the greased ovenproof dishes and slightly smooth the surface of each soufflé.

4 Place the dishes in a baking dish and pour in enough hot water to come halfway up the sides of the dishes. Cook for 20 minutes, or until well puffed and golden. Remove the dishes from the water and stand for 5 minutes (they will deflate and look wrinkled).

5 Gently ease the soufflés out of the moulds and into individual shallow oven proof dishes, then pour over the combined cream and Vermouth. Return to the oven for a further 15 minutes. When re-puffed and light golden, remove from the oven and serve immediately with the caramelised pears.

CHOCOLATE MOUSSE CAKE
WITH POACHED PEARS AND CRÈME FRAÎCHE

PREP 30 MINS + OVERNIGHT REFRIGERATION COOK 1 HOUR 40 MINS SERVES 8

340g dark chocolate, broken into small pieces
225g unsalted butter, softened
5 eggs
340g caster sugar

POACHED PEARS

4 Beurre Bosc pears, peeled, cored and halved
1 cinnamon stick, broken into pieces
100g brown sugar

crème fraîche, to serve
½ teaspoon black salt, to garnish
extra cocoa, for dusting
mint leaves, to garnish

1. Preheat the oven to 180°C. To prepare the pears, place in a small casserole dish and add the cinnamon, sugar and enough boiling water to cover the pears. Cover with foil and cook in the oven for about 40 minutes or until very tender. Remove the pears and set aside to cool. Refrigerate, covered, until required.
2. To prepare the cake, preheat the oven to 160°C. Grease a 22cm round springform tin and line the base and sides with baking paper.
3. Melt the chocolate and butter in a medium heatproof bowl over a saucepan of simmering water, stirring to combine. Remove from the heat and cool for 10 minutes.
4. Whisk together the eggs and sugar until pale and creamy. Fold half the cooled chocolate mixture into the egg and sugar mixture, then repeat with the remaining batch.
5. Pour the mixture into the prepared tin. Place in a roasting pan and add enough boiling water to come halfway up the sides of the cake pan. Cook in the centre of the oven for 55 minutes. Remove the cake pan from the roasting dish, set aside to cool and refrigerate overnight.
6. To serve, remove the outer ring of the pan and cut the cake into generous slices. Place each slice on a serving plate, spoon over a generous amount of crème fraîche and garnish with black salt. Place a pear half beside each slice of cake, dust over a little cocoa and garnish with fresh mint.

If black salt is unavailable, try garnishing the crème fraîche with a little grated chocolate.

These doughnuts would be great served with a chocolate sauce. Place 200g finely chopped dark chocolate in a heatproof bowl. Heat 200ml thickened cream in a small saucepan until hot. Pour over the chocolate, stand for 1 minute and mix until smooth.

ZEPPOLE
(ITALIAN POTATO DOUGHNUTS)

PREP 30 MINS + 30 MINS STANDING COOK 10 MINS MAKES ABOUT 20

300g plain flour (preferably Italian '00')
50g caster sugar
15g dried yeast
250g Desiree potatoes, peeled
25g butter
1 egg
125ml warm milk
2 tsp ground cinnamon
100g caster sugar, extra
vegetable oil, for deep-frying

1. Combine the flour, sugar and yeast in a small bowl. Set aside.
2. Place the potatoes in a saucepan of cold salted water. Bring to the boil and boil gently until tender. Drain and push through a ricer into a bowl.
3. While the potatoes are still warm, add the flour mixture, butter, egg and warm milk. Using your hands, bring all the ingredients together to form a soft dough.
4. Roll walnut-sized balls of the dough into 10cm-long sausages. Shape the sausages into a doughnut. Place on a floured tray, 3cm apart. Stand, covered, in a warm place for 30 minutes, or until double in size.
5. Combine the cinnamon and extra sugar in a shallow bowl.
6. Fill a deep-fryer or large saucepan one-third full with vegetable oil and heat over medium heat to 180°C (or until a cube of bread turns golden in 10 seconds). Deep-fry the doughnuts in small batches. Drain on paper towel, roll in cinnamon sugar and serve.

SPICED COFFEE-SOAKED DATES
WITH SESAME AND CINNAMON COOKIES

PREP 1 HOUR COOK 30 MINS SERVES 4

12 pitted dates

SESAME AND CINNAMON COOKIES

50g butter, at room temperature
55g caster sugar
55g brown sugar
1 tsp vanilla extract
1 egg
100g self-raising flour
a pinch of salt
1 tbsp sesame seeds
2 tsp ground cinnamon

SPICED COFFEE

3 tbsp coffee beans
5 cardamom pods, crushed
2 tsp ground nutmeg
a pinch of ground cloves
1 tsp ground ginger
1 tbsp caster sugar
2 tbsp coffee-flavoured liqueur

toasted walnuts and whipped cream, to serve

1. To make the cookies, preheat the oven to 190°C. Line two oven trays with baking paper.
2. Beat the butter, sugars and vanilla extract until fluffy. Beat in the egg, then fold in the combined flour and salt.
3. Roll teaspoons of the mixture into balls. Lightly flatten the balls into 4cm rounds. Place on the prepared tray 4cm apart. Sprinkle with sesame seeds and cinnamon. Cook for 6 minutes until golden. Allow to cool on the trays.
4. To make the spiced coffee, grind the coffee beans and spices using a mortar and pestle or a coffee grinder until fine. Add the mixture to a coffee percolator or plunger with 600ml water and percolate.
5. Transfer the coffee mixture to a saucepan with the sugar. Simmer, stirring occasionally, for 5 minutes to further infuse the flavours. Stir in the liqueur and remove from the heat.
6. Place the dates in a small bowl. Add half the coffee mixture and stand, covered, for at least 30 minutes. Strain.
7. Reheat the remaining coffee mixture. Serve the dates with whipped cream, nuts and cookies and a shot of the remaining coffee on the side.

If you don't have a coffee grinder, add pre-ground spices to 600ml of freshly made coffee. Simmer and strain through muslin before adding the liqueur.

SAKE FIGS

PREP 30 MINS COOK 15 MINS SERVES 4

SESAME BALLS

40g brown sugar
100ml boiling water, plus 60ml to dip
125g glutinous rice flour
½ tsp baking powder
sesame seeds, for coating
vegetable oil, for deep-frying

SAKE SAUTÉED FIGS

125ml sake
75g brown sugar
1 cinnamon quill
1 star anise
finely grated zest and juice of 1 lemon
4 firm ripe figs, halved

double cream, to serve

1. To make the sesame balls, stir the sugar and water in a jug until the sugar has dissolved.
2. Combine the flour and baking powder in a medium bowl. Stir in the sugar mixture to form a soft dough. Roll teaspoons of the mixture into balls. Briefly dip the balls in water and roll in sesame seeds to coat.
3. Fill a large saucepan or wok one-third full with vegetable oil and heat over medium heat to 180°C (or until a cube of bread turns golden in 10 seconds). Deep-fry the sesame balls in small batches for 5 minutes, or until golden brown, expanded and cooked through. To achieve even cooking and colour, you will need to press the balls against the side of the pan or wok to rotate them during cooking. Drain on paper towel.
4. To make the figs, stir the sake, sugar, cinnamon and star anise in a small, deep frying pan until the sugar has dissolved. Stir in the lemon zest and juice. Simmer the liquid slightly for 5 minutes, or until reduced to a thin syrup. Remove from heat and place figs cut side down in syrup at room temperature for 3 minutes.
5. Serve the figs and syrup with the sesame balls and whipped cream.

BLUEBERRY BRIOCHE CUP
WITH LABNEH

PREP 30 MINS + REFRIGERATION COOK 15 MINS SERVES 4

butter or oil, to grease
55g plain flour
1½ tbsp caster sugar
¾ tsp cinnamon
280ml milk
4 eggs
¼ tsp vanilla bean paste
75g brioche, cut into 1cm cubes
125g blueberries
60g cream cheese, diced

LABNEH

¼ tsp salt
280ml Greek yoghurt

BLUEBERRY COULIS

250g blueberries
110g sugar
juice of ½ lemon
1 tsp cornflour
1 tsp water

ALMOND TOPPING

40g flaked almonds
1 tbsp caster sugar
¼ tsp cinnamon

TOFFEE BLUEBERRIES

110g sugar
60ml water
12 blueberries

1 To make the *labneh*, line a sieve with muslin and place over a bowl. Stir the salt into the yoghurt and pour the yoghurt into the sieve, then refrigerate for several hours or overnight to drain.

2 To make the blueberry coulis, stir the blueberries, sugar and lemon juice in a small saucepan over medium heat until the sugar has dissolved. Simmer over low heat for 10 minutes, or until the blueberries are soft. Cool slightly, then push through a sieve. Return to a clean saucepan and stir in the combined cornflour and water. Bring to the boil and simmer for 5–10 minutes, or until thickened. Set aside to cool completely.

3 To make the almond topping, combine the almonds, sugar and cinnamon in a small bowl.

4 To make the brioche cups, preheat the oven to 200°C. Grease 4 (180ml) holes of a muffin pan. Sift the flour, sugar and cinnamon into a medium bowl. Whisk in the combined milk, eggs and vanilla bean paste to form a batter. Divide the brioche and half the blueberries among the prepared pan holes. Pour in the batter, top with cream cheese and the remaining blueberries, then sprinkle with the almond topping and bake for 15 minutes, or until golden brown.

5 Meanwhile, to make the toffee blueberries, line an oven tray with baking paper. Stir the sugar and water in a small, heavy-based saucepan over medium heat, without boiling, until the sugar has dissolved. Use a wet pastry brush to brush any stray grains on the side of the pan back down into the mixture. Bring to the boil and boil, uncovered and without stirring, for 10–15 minutes, or until the mixture turns golden brown. Remove from the heat and, using a toothpick, dip the blueberries into the toffee, then place on the prepared tray for 5 minutes to set.

6 Place the brioche cups on serving plates and top with the toffee blueberries. Serve with the *labneh* and coulis.

The tarts can be made and filled with syrup and pastry cream several hours in advance. Store, covered, in the refrigerator. Bring to room temperature and top with the freshly cooked bananas to serve.

BANANA TARTLETS
WITH MASCARPONE CREAM AND PRALINE

PREP 30 MINS + 1 HOUR 30 MINS REFRIGERATION COOK 40 MINS SERVES 4

1 tsp Bundaberg rum
250g mascarpone
4 tsp golden syrup

PASTRY

125g unsalted butter, chopped, at room temperature
50g caster sugar
1 egg, lightly beaten
250g plain flour, sifted
a pinch of salt

PASTRY CREAM

250ml milk
1¼ tsp vanilla bean paste
40g caster sugar
20g cornflour
2 egg yolks
a pinch of salt

MACADAMIA PRALINE

25g macadamia nuts, toasted and finely chopped
100g sugar
50ml water

CARAMELISED BANANA

20g unsalted butter
10g brown sugar
2 firm ripe bananas, peeled and cut into 5mm slices

raspberries, to serve

1 To make the pastry, beat the butter and sugar with an electric mixer until lightly creamed, then gradually drizzle in the egg until combined. Stir in the flour and salt until the mixture just comes together to form a dough. Cover in cling film and refrigerate for at least 90 minutes.

2 Meanwhile, gently stir the rum into the mascarpone and refrigerate until required.

3 To make the pastry cream, heat the milk and vanilla bean paste in a heavy-based saucepan over medium heat, without boiling, until hot. Remove from the heat.

4 Whisk the sugar, cornflour, egg yolks, salt and 60ml of the milk mixture in a medium bowl to form a smooth paste. Gradually whisk in the remaining milk mixture. Transfer the mixture to the same saucepan and cook over medium heat, stirring continuously, for 2–3 minutes, or until thickened. Pass through a coarse strainer or sieve into a large bowl, then cover with cling film and refrigerate until cold.

5 Preheat the oven to 180°C. Lightly grease 4 x 8cm-round loose-based tart pans.

6 Roll out the dough between 2 sheets of baking paper until 3mm thick. Cut out 4 x 11cm rounds and use to line the prepared pans. Roll a rolling pin over the tops of the pans to trim the edges and prick the bases with a fork. Reserve the remaining pastry for another use.

7 Bake for 11–12 minutes, or until golden, then cool completely. Spread the base of each tart shell with 1 teaspoon of golden syrup. Beat the pastry cream vigorously to loosen, then pipe or spoon into the tart shells.

continued next page ➤

BANANA TARTLETS

WITH MASCARPONE CREAM AND PRALINE

(continued)

8 Meanwhile, to make the praline, line an oven tray with baking paper. Spread the nuts on the tray in a single layer. Stir the sugar and water in a medium-sized heavy-based saucepan over medium heat, without boiling, until the sugar has dissolved. Use a wet pastry brush to brush down any stray sugar crystals on the side of the pan. Bring the mixture to the boil and boil, without stirring, for 7–8 minutes, or until golden brown. Carefully pour the caramel over the nuts on the prepared tray. Cool until set, then break into pieces and process in a food processor until coarsely chopped.

9 To make the caramelised bananas, melt the butter and sugar in a frying pan over medium heat. Add the bananas and cook, turning occasionally, for 5–10 minutes, or until golden brown.

10 To serve, place the tarts on four serving plates and top with the bananas. Serve with mascarpone, praline and raspberries.

MACARONS SIX WAYS

PREP 2 HOURS   COOK 1 HOUR   MAKES 24

fresh blueberries, to decorate
fresh raspberries, to decorate

MACARONS

200g caster sugar
75ml water
4 egg whites
200g almond meal, sifted
200g icing sugar, sifted
gel food colouring in orange, blue, purple, red, yellow and brown

BUTTERCREAM

180g caster sugar
125ml water
3 egg yolks
300g unsalted butter, diced and softened

MANGO FLAVOURING

1 small mango, deseeded, peeled and flesh puréed

BLUEBERRY FLAVOURING

2 tsp blueberry jam

PISTACHIO FLAVOURING

a drop of almond essence
¼ cup pistachios, finely chopped, to serve

RASPBERRY COULIS

100g frozen raspberries
50g caster sugar
1 tsp lemon juice

CHOCOLATE GANACHE

200g dark chocolate, chopped
100ml thickened cream
1 tbsp rum (optional)

LEMON CURD

75g cornflour
220g caster sugar
125ml lemon juice
310ml water
2 tsp grated lemon zest
3 egg yolks
60g unsalted butter, chopped

1 To make the macarons, preheat the oven to 180°C. Combine the caster sugar and water in a small saucepan and simmer over low heat, stirring, for 8–10 minutes, or until the sugar has dissolved. Heat the sugar syrup until it reaches 118°C (test using a sugar thermometer), brushing down the sides with a wet pastry brush to avoid crystallisation.

2 Meanwhile, using an electric mixer on medium speed, whisk 2 egg whites in a medium bowl until soft peaks form. Increase the speed to high, then slowly add the hot sugar syrup in a constant stream until combined. Set aside.

3 Combine the almond meal and icing sugar in a medium stainless-steel bowl, then gradually add the remaining unbeaten egg whites, mixing with a wooden spoon until the mixture is firm and paste-like.

4 Separate the mixture into 6 smaller bowls – one per colour. (In this recipe we are making 6 different colours.) Add the desired food colouring to each bowl and combine well, then divide the beaten egg white and sugar syrup mixture evenly between each bowl and thoroughly combine. The mixtures should have a velvety texture.

5 Spoon the coloured mixtures into piping bags fitted with a 1cm plain nozzle. Pipe the mixture to make 3cm rounds on silicon-mat-lined baking trays. Tap the trays to flatten the peaks and rest for 30 minutes, or until the mixture feels dry to the touch and forms a skin.

6 Reduce the oven temperature to 150°C and place the trays in the oven. Bake for 15 minutes, or until the bases are firm and a macaron can be lifted from the tray. Remove the trays from the oven and allow to cool on the tray.

continued next page ➤

MACARONS SIX WAYS
(continued)

7 To make the buttercream, place the sugar and water in a small saucepan over medium heat and stir for 8–10 minutes, or until the sugar has dissolved. Brush the sides of the saucepan with a wet pastry brush to avoid crystallisation. Boil to 121°C (test using a sugar thermometer).

8 Meanwhile, using an electric mixer on high speed, whisk the egg yolks in a medium bowl until thick and pale. Reduce the speed to medium and gradually pour in the sugar syrup in a thin, steady stream. Whisk for 5 minutes, then add the butter one piece at a time, whisking after each addition, until combined. Divide the mixture between 6 bowls to make the different-flavoured fillings and leave for 15–20 minutes to cool completely.

9 For the mango filling, add the mango purée to the buttercream to taste and mix thoroughly. For the blueberry filling, add the blueberry jam to the buttercream and mix thoroughly. For the pistachio filling, add a drop of essence to the buttercream. Add extra to taste if desired.

10 To make the raspberry coulis, place the raspberries, sugar and lemon juice in a medium-sized saucepan over low heat for 8–10 minutes, or until the sugar has dissolved and the mixture is smooth, then strain through a fine sieve into a small bowl and set aside to cool. When ready, add to the buttercream, 1 teaspoon at a time, to taste.

11 To make the lemon curd, combine the cornflour and sugar in a medium-sized saucepan over low heat, then gradually stir in the lemon juice and water until smooth. Cook for 3–5 minutes, or until the mixture boils and thickens. Remove from the heat and stir in the lemon zest, egg yolks and butter. Stir until melted. Cover with cling film and cool to room temperature. When ready, add to the buttercream, 1 teaspoon at a time, to taste.

12 To make the ganache, melt the chocolate in a heatproof bowl over a saucepan of simmering water until smooth. Add the cream and rum, if using, and stir until thickened, then cool to set. When ready, add to the buttercream, 1 teaspoon at a time, to taste.

13 To assemble the macarons, pipe the mango filling between the orange macarons and blueberry filling between blue macarons. For the pistachio filling, pipe between the purple macarons, then roll the sides in pistachios. Pipe the raspberry filling between the red macarons, lemon curd between the yellow macarons and ganache between the brown macarons. Sandwich the macarons together and top the blue macarons with a blueberry and the red macarons with a raspberry, using a little extra filling to secure.

Macarons are tricky to make, and your kitchen's humidity and temperature can make a big difference. Try to prepare them in a cool environment. The macarons must form a skin before going into the oven, so make sure you allow time for them to rest properly.

If you don't have a silicone mat, you can cook the cake in a greased and lined 20cm × 30cm slice pan.

SEASON 3 · LEIGH & JENNIFER

CHOCOLATE HAZELNUT CAKE

PREP 3 HOURS + SETTING TIME COOK 1 HOUR 30 MINUTES MAKES 6

CAKE

100g dark chocolate (70% cocoa), chopped
100g unsalted butter
80g sugar
2 eggs
25g plain flour

CHOCOLATE MOUSSE

100g dark chocolate (70% cocoa), chopped
1 egg, separated
80ml thickened cream
1 tbsp caster sugar

CARAMEL CREAM

50g caster sugar
1 tbsp water
200ml thickened cream
50g milk chocolate, chopped
¼ tsp sea salt
200ml double cream

HAZELNUT PRALINE

30g sugar
20g roasted hazelnuts, finely chopped

GANACHE

25g caster sugar
2 tsp water
60ml thickened cream
60g unsalted butter
30g dark chocolate (80% cocoa)
30g smooth hazelnut chocolate

CHERRY JAM

20g sugar
80ml cherry purée
½ tsp xanthan gum

CHOCOLATE ALMOND PRALINE

100g caster sugar
1 tbsp water
80g blanched almonds, roasted
100g white chocolate, melted

dark chocolate crunchy pearls, to decorate
edible violets, to decorate

1. To make the cake, preheat the oven to 180°C. Place a silicone mat on an oven tray. Melt the chocolate in a heatproof bowl over a saucepan of simmering water until smooth.
2. Beat the butter and sugar with an electric mixer until pale and fluffy. Add the eggs one at a time, beating between additions. Add the melted chocolate and beat until combined. Fold in the flour.
3. Thinly spread the mixture onto the silicone mat until about 5mm thick. Bake for 5 minutes, or until the cake springs back when touched. Allow to cool, then, using an 8cm-round cookie cutter, cut out 6 rounds.
4. To make the chocolate mousse, melt the chocolate in a heatproof bowl over a saucepan of simmering water until smooth. Whisk the egg white until soft peaks form. Beat the cream with an electric mixer until soft peaks form. Whisk the egg yolks and sugar in a small heatproof bowl over a saucepan of simmering water until thick and creamy. Remove from the heat, then fold in the melted chocolate. Fold in the cream, then fold in the egg white. Refrigerate for 2 hours, or until firm.
5. To make the caramel cream, stir the sugar and water in a small saucepan over low heat until sugar has dissolved. Cook over low heat, without stirring, for approximately 5–10 minutes, or until it turns dark golden. Add the thickened cream (the caramel may harden at this point). Stir over low heat until the mixture has melted and combined. Remove from the heat and stir in the chocolate and salt until melted and smooth. Allow to cool slightly. Set aside and refrigerate 4 tablespoons of this caramel cream to decorate the cakes.
6. Lightly whisk the double cream to form soft peaks. Fold into the cooled caramel cream mixture. Refrigerate for 2 hours, or until firm.

continued next page ➤

CHOCOLATE HAZELNUT CAKE
(continued)

7 To make the hazelnut praline, line a tray with baking paper. Heat the sugar in a small saucepan over low heat, without stirring, or until it has melted. Continue cooking over low heat without stirring for 5 minutes, or until golden. Quickly stir in the nuts to coat evenly, then pour onto the prepared tray. Set aside for 5 minutes to set, then process in a food processor to form coarse crumbs.

8 To make the ganache, stir the sugar and water in a small saucepan over low heat until the sugar has dissolved. Continue cooking, without stirring, for 5–10 minutes, or until the mixture turns dark golden. Add the cream (the caramel may harden at this point) and whisk until smooth and combined. Add the butter and chocolate and stir until smooth and combined. Remove from the heat. Refrigerate for about 2 hours, or until firm.

9 To make the cherry jam, stir the sugar and purée in a small saucepan over medium heat until the sugar has dissolved. Add the xanthan gum and stir for 5–10 minutes, or until thickened. Strain and allow to cool.

10 To make the chocolate almond praline, line a tray with baking paper. Stir the sugar and water in a small saucepan over low heat until the sugar has dissolved. Continue cooking, without stirring, for 5–10 minutes, or until the mixture turns dark golden. Quickly stir in the almonds to coat evenly, then pour the mixture onto the prepared tray. Set aside for 5 minutes to set. Pour over the white chocolate. Allow to set, then process in a food processor to form coarse crumbs.

11 To assemble the cake, place the cake rounds in the bases of 6 8cm-round, 2½ cm-high presentation rings. Add the mousse and spread up to the rim of the ring, leaving an indent in the centre for the fillings. Sprinkle a little praline in the centre, then top with a teaspoon of the ganache. Spread the top with caramel cream (to fill the remaining indent) and level with a palette knife. Refrigerate for two hours, or until set. To remove the cakes, run a knife around the inside of the ring to loosen (you can use a blow torch to gently heat the outside of the ring if you have one).

12 To serve, paint cherry jam across length of 6 plates. Place the cake in the centre and top with a dollop of the reserved chocolate caramel mixture. Add a sprinkle of chocolate almond praline and top with chocolate pearls and edible violets.

CHOCOLATE RASPBERRY POP DELIGHT

PREP 3 HOURS + SETTING TIME COOK 40 MINS SERVES 4

100g dark cooking chocolate, melted

BISCUIT BASE

60g Arnott's Choc Ripple biscuits
20g unsalted butter, melted

CHOCOLATE MOUSSE

50g dark chocolate (70% cocoa)
1 egg
30g caster sugar
150ml thickened cream
1 tsp vanilla extract
¾ tsp powdered gelatine
2 tbsp chocolate popping candy

RASPBERRY MOUSSE

1 egg
30g caster sugar
2 tsp raspberry liqueur
½ tsp raspberry essence
½ tsp pink food colouring
150ml thickened cream
¾ tsp gelatine powder

RASPBERRY COULIS

100g frozen raspberries
50g sugar
2 tsp lemon juice

CHOCOLATE RASPBERRY MACARONS

80g egg whites
10g caster sugar
2 tbsp water
100g almond meal
100g icing sugar mixture
red gel food colouring

MACARON FILLING

250g dark chocolate (70%)
50g dark chocolate (50%)
150ml thickened cream
2 tbsp raspberry jam

raspberries and sliced strawberries, to serve

1 Place 5 perspex tubes (see note page 191) on a tray lined with baking paper.

2 To make the biscuit base, process the biscuits and butter to form crumbs. Divide among the perspex tubes, pressing over the base.

3 To make the chocolate mousse, melt the chocolate in a heatproof bowl over a saucepan of simmering water until smooth. Remove from the heat and allow to cool slightly. Beat the egg and sugar in a small bowl with an electric mixer until pale and thick. Add the cream and vanilla and beat until thick. Add the melted chocolate and beat until combined. Dissolve the gelatine in 2 teaspoons of hot water (not boiling) and stir into the mousse mixture. Divide the mousse among the tubes over the biscuit base. Sprinkle with popping candy and refrigerate.

4 To make the raspberry mousse, beat the egg and sugar in a small bowl with an electric mixer until pale and thick. Add the liqueur, essence and colouring and beat to combine. Add the cream and beat until thick. Dissolve the gelatine in 2 teaspoons of hot water (not boiling) and stir into mousse. Divide the mousse among the perspex tubes over the chocolate layer. Refrigerate for several hours, or overnight.

5 To make the coulis, combine all the ingredients in a small saucepan over low heat. Stir until the sugar has dissolved and the mixture is soft. Push through a fine sieve.

6 When the mousses have set, cut the tape and peel away the perspex.

7 To make the chocolate-lace collars for the mousse, drizzle the remaining strips of perspex widthways with melted chocolate. Wrap around the mousse, chocolate-side in, and secure with sticky tape. Refrigerate for 30 minutes, or until set. Gently cut the tape and remove the perspex.

continued next page ➤

CHOCOLATE RASPBERRY POP DELIGHT
(continued)

8 To make the macarons, line two oven trays with silicone mats or baking paper. Beat half the egg whites with an electric mixer to form soft peaks. Stir the sugar and water in a small saucepan until the sugar has dissolved and forms a syrup. Bring to 118°C (test using a sugar thermometer).

9 With the electric mixer motor running, gradually add the hot sugar syrup to the beaten egg whites in a thin steady stream to form a thick, glossy meringue.

10 Sift the almond meal and icing sugar into a metal bowl then stir in the remaining egg whites. Fold the mixture into the meringue in two batches, then fold in enough food colouring to tint the mixture pink.

11 Using a piping bag fitted with a 1cm nozzle, pipe the mixture into 3cm rounds on the prepared trays. Stand at room temperature for 30 minutes, or until the mixture feels dry to touch and has formed a skin.

12 Meanwhile, preheat the oven to 200°C. Reduce the temperature to 150°C and place the trays in the oven. Bake for 15 minutes, or until the bases are firm and a macaron can be lifted from the tray. Remove the trays from the oven and allow to cool on the tray.

13 To make the macaron filling, stir all the ingredients in a heatproof bowl over a saucepan of simmering water until smooth and combined. Refrigerate for 30 minutes, or until thick enough to spread or pipe. Sandwich the macarons with filling.

14 To serve, place the mousse in the centre of 4 plates, each with 1 macaron. Dot the plate with coulis and garnish with a raspberry and sliced strawberry.

Gel or paste food colouring is a highly concentrated form of colouring. It is available from cake decorating suppliers and specialty stores. You will need eight 5cm × 23cm pieces of food-grade perspex to make this recipe. Roll half the pieces to form four 6cm-diameter tubes for the mousse. Secure with sticky tape. The remaining pieces can be left flat to make the chocolate lace collars.

If peaches are not in season, try topping the pannacotta with fresh berries.

YOGHURT PANNACOTTA

WITH LEMON ZEST JELLY, WHITE PEACHES AND THYME SYRUP

PREP 45 MINS + 4 HOURS SETTING TIME   COOK 30 MINS   SERVES 4

2 white peaches, halved, cored and thinly sliced

PANNACOTTA

olive oil cooking spray
300ml pure cream
110g caster sugar
1 vanilla bean, split and seeds scraped
2 titanium-strength gelatine leaves, soaked in water
250ml plain Greek yoghurt

THYME SYRUP

125ml lemon juice
165g (½ cup) caster sugar
3 thyme sprigs
zest of ½ lemon

LEMON JELLY

finely grated zest of 1 lemon
125ml water
2 tsp caster sugar
½ tsp powdered agar agar

1 To make the pannacotta, lightly grease a 20cm x 20cm pan with cooking spray. Place the cream, sugar and vanilla bean and seeds in a large saucepan over medium heat and stir for 4–5 minutes, or until the sugar has dissolved. Remove from the heat, remove the vanilla bean and set aside.

2 Squeeze out the excess water from the gelatine leaves, then add to the cream mixture and whisk until dissolved. Whisk in the yoghurt. Pour into the prepared pan and refrigerate for 4 hours, or until set.

3 To make the thyme syrup, place the lemon juice, sugar and thyme in a small saucepan over low–medium heat and stir for 6–8 minutes, or until the sugar has dissolved. Add the lemon zest and stir to combine. Remove from the heat and set aside.

4 To make the lemon jelly, sprinkle the grated zest evenly over a 30cm x 20cm baking tray lined with baking paper. Stir the water, sugar and agar agar in a saucepan over medium heat until boiling. Pour the mixture over the lemon zest on the mat. Spread evenly using a palette knife. Allow to cool for 10 minutes, or until set.

5 Invert the pannacotta onto a chopping board. Using an 8cm square cutter, cut out four squares. Using a spatula, gently transfer to serving plates. Cut out squares of lemon jelly with the same cutter and, using a palette knife, place on top of the pannacotta. Top with sliced peaches and drizzle with strained syrup.

STRAWBERRY AND AMARETTO SEMIFREDDO

PREP 2 HOURS + REFRIGERATION TIME COOK 30 MINS SERVES 6

vegetable oil, for deep-frying

SEMIFREDDO

4 egg yolks
150g caster sugar
1 tbsp Amaretto
1 vanilla bean, split and seeds scraped
300ml thickened cream
100g crème fraîche
150g strawberries, hulled and halved

STRAWBERRY GELÉE

500g strawberries, hulled and chopped
55g sugar
7g agar agar powder

AMARETTO SYRUP

110g caster sugar
125ml water
2 tbsp Amaretto

MACERATED STRAWBERRIES

250g strawberries, hulled, chopped
¼ cup finely chopped basil
2 tbsp caster sugar

CROSTOLI

300g plain flour, plus extra, to dust
zest of 1 lemon
100g softened butter
2 eggs
1 egg yolk
a pinch of salt
50g caster sugar
50ml Marsala

icing sugar, to dust

1 To make the semifreddo, place the egg yolks, sugar, Amaretto and vanilla seeds in a large heatproof bowl over a large saucepan of simmering water. Whisk with a handheld electric mixer for 15 minutes, or until mixture has tripled in size. Set aside for 5 minutes.

2 Meanwhile, using an electric mixer, beat the cream and crème fraîche in a medium bowl until soft peaks form.

3 Add the cream mixture and strawberries to the egg yolk mixture and fold to combine. Divide the mixture among 6 serving glasses roughly ¾ cup in size. Freeze for 3 hours, or until frozen.

4 To make the gelée, process the strawberries and sugar in a food processor until smooth. Place the mixture with agar agar in a medium-sized saucepan over low heat and cook, stirring, for 2 minutes, or until the sugar has dissolved, then continue to cook for a further 1 minute, or until thickened. Pour onto a 20 x 30cm baking tray lined with baking paper and allow to cool. Use a cookie cutter to cut out 6 rounds to fit your serving glasses.

5 Meanwhile, to make the Amaretto syrup, place the sugar and water in a small saucepan over medium heat and cook, stirring, for 5 minutes, or until the sugar has dissolved. Reduce the heat to low and cook for a further 3 minutes, or until thickened. Remove from the heat and stir in the Amaretto.

6 To macerate the strawberries, place all the ingredients in a medium bowl and stir to combine. Cover and refrigerate for 1 hour.

7 To make the crostoli, place the flour on a work surface and create a well in the centre. Add the remaining ingredients to the flour and knead to form a smooth dough. Wrap the dough in cling film and set aside for 1 hour. Using a pasta machine, roll the dough until 5mm thick, then cut into 2cm x 10cm pieces. Fill a saucepan or deep-fryer one-third full with vegetable oil and place over medium heat until hot. Deep-fry the dough in batches for 2 minutes, or until golden and crisp. Remove with a slotted spoon and drain on paper towel, then dust with icing sugar.

8 To serve, place the gelée circles on top of the semifreddo. Top with macerated strawberries and drizzle with syrup. Serve with crostoli.

Isomalt is a type of sugar that does not colour when cooked. It is available from specialist cake decorating shops. If you are short on time you could use and flavour ready-made fondant and boiled mint lollies to make the mint crumble.

SEASON 4 · DAN & STEPH

CHOCOLATE PEPPERMINT DELICE

PREP 30 MINS + COOLING TIME 1 HOUR   COOK 1 HOUR 30 MINS   SERVES 6

CHOCOLATE MOUSSE
120ml milk
275ml cream
300g dark chocolate (70% cocoa), chopped
2 eggs, lightly beaten

CHOCOLATE CAKE
180g dark chocolate (70% cocoa), chopped
180g unsalted butter
3 eggs
250g caster sugar
1 tsp vanilla extract
110g plain flour
½ tsp salt

MINT FONDANT
500g icing sugar mixture
2 small egg whites
2 tbsp liquid glucose
1–2 drops peppermint essence

PEPPERMINT CRUMBLE
2 cups isomalt
2 drops peppermint oil

CRÈME DE MENTHE CREAM
800ml thickened cream
2 tbsp icing sugar
60ml crème de menthe
1 drop peppermint oil

melted chocolate, to serve
baby mint leaves, to decorate

1 Preheat the oven to 110°C. Line a 20cm x 20cm baking pan with baking paper.

2 To make the chocolate mousse, place the milk and cream in a saucepan over low heat and simmer for 3–4 minutes. Place the chocolate in a large bowl and pour over the hot milk mixture. Allow to stand for 1 minute, then whisk until smooth and combined. Set aside to cool slightly, then beat in the eggs. Pour into the prepared pan and bake for 30 minutes (it should still have a slight wobble in the centre). Remove from the oven and cool to room temperature then refrigerate for 1 hour. Remove from the pan and cut into six rectangles.

3 To make the chocolate cake, increase the oven temperature to 180°C. Grease a 20cm x 20cm baking pan and line with baking paper. Stir the chocolate and butter in a heatproof bowl over a saucepan of simmering water until smooth and combined.

4 In a separate medium bowl, beat the eggs, sugar and vanilla together until light and doubled in size. Add to the chocolate mixture and whisk to combine, then stir in the combined sifted flour and salt. Pour into the prepared dish and bake for 30 minutes, or until a skewer inserted in the centre of the cake comes out clean. Remove from the oven and cool to room temperature. Remove from the pan and cut into 6 rectangles, trim rough edges and even top of the cake.

5 To make the mint fondant, combine all the ingredients in a medium bowl to form a smooth dough. Turn the dough out onto a surface dusted with icing sugar. Knead for 5 minutes. Using a rolling pin dusted with icing sugar, roll out the dough into a 20cm square. Cut into 6 rectangles.

continued next page ➤

CHOCOLATE PEPPERMINT DELICE

(continued)

6 To make the peppermint crumble, place the isomalt in a small saucepan over low heat and stir for 5 minutes. Increase the heat to medium and bring the mixture to 175°C (test using a sugar thermometer). Add the peppermint oil and stir to combine. Pour the mixture onto a silicone mat and set aside until cool enough to touch. Knead and stretch the mixture until it becomes opaque and hard. Break into small pieces, then process in a food processor until crumbs form.

7 To make the crème de menthe cream, beat all the ingredients until firm peaks form.

8 To assemble, brush the melted chocolate onto 6 plates. Place the fondant on the plates, then layer with the cake and mousse. Sprinkle with mint crumble and add a quenelle of crème de menthe cream. Decorate with baby mint leaves and serve.

RED VELVET WITH CHOCOLATE AND RASPBERRIES

PREP 2 HOURS + FREEZING   COOK 55 MINS   SERVES 10–12

150ml thickened cream, whipped to soft peaks
fresh raspberries, to serve

SEMIFREDDO

3 large eggs
2 egg yolks
150g caster sugar
1 tsp vanilla extract
500ml thickened cream
6 raspberries, crushed with a fork
pink food colouring, to tint

RASPBERRY JELLY

750ml raspberry juice
7 sheets gold-strength leaf gelatine leaves (2g each)

CHOCOLATE GANACHE

170ml thickened cream
400g dark chocolate, finely chopped

RED VELVET CAKE

125g butter, softened
330g caster sugar
2 large eggs, at room temperature
1½ tsp vanilla extract
275ml buttermilk
250g plain flour
2 tbsp Dutch cocoa powder
1 tsp salt
1 tsp bicarbonate of soda
1 tsp apple cider vinegar
red food colouring, to tint

RASPBERRY COULIS

250g frozen raspberries
55g (¼ cup) caster sugar

1 To make the semifreddo, whisk the eggs, yolks, sugar and vanilla together in a heatproof bowl until combined. Place the bowl over a saucepan of simmering water for 6–7 minutes, or until the mixture is thick, pale and almost tripled in volume. Remove from the heat and allow to cool slightly.

2 Beat the cream until soft peaks form. Fold into the egg mixture in two batches, then fold in the raspberries. Tint the mixture pink with food colouring. Pour into a freezer-proof container and freeze for several hours or overnight.

3 To make the jelly, line a 20cm x 30cm slice pan with cling film, overhanging on all sides, and soak the gelatine leaves in cold water until soft.

4 Heat half the juice in a saucepan over medium heat until hot, then remove from the heat. Squeeze excess water out of the gelatine and add to the hot juice. Stir until dissolved, then stir in the remaining juice. Strain into the prepared pan and refrigerate until set.

5 To make the ganache, line a 20cm square cake pan with cling film, overhanging on all sides.

6 Heat the cream in a saucepan until hot, then remove from the heat. Add the chocolate and stand for 2 minutes. Stir until smooth and combined. Pour into prepared pan and refrigerate for several hours or until firm and set. Using a knife dipped in hot water and then dried, cut the ganache into 12 squares.

7 To make the cake, preheat the oven to 180°C and grease a 20cm x 30cm slice pan. Line the base and sides with baking paper. Using an electric mixer, beat the butter and sugar until pale and fluffy. Beat in the eggs one at a time, then beat in the vanilla. Alternately, beat in the buttermilk and combined sifted flour, cocoa, salt and bicarbonate of soda in two batches. Stir in the vinegar and enough food colouring to tint the mixture dark red. Pour into the prepared pan.

8 Bake for 25–30 minutes, or until a skewer comes out clean when inserted in the centre. Cool for 5 minutes in the pan, then invert onto a wire rack to cool completely.

continued next page ➤

RED VELVET WITH CHOCOLATE AND RASPBERRIES
(continued)

9 To make the coulis, stir the raspberries and sugar in a saucepan over medium heat until the sugar has dissolved, the raspberries are broken down and the mixture is soft. Simmer for 5 minutes. Pass through a sieve and refrigerate until cold.

10 To assemble, place the cake on top of the jelly in the pan. Invert the whole thing onto a chopping board, so you have a layer of cake topped with a layer of jelly. Cut into rectangles.

11 Serve the jelly-topped cake with the ganache and a dollop of whipped cream, fresh raspberries and semifreddo.

Raspberry juice is available from grocers and delicatessens. If unavailable, you can use a combination of cranberry and raspberry, which is available in supermarkets. Alternatively, you can use a combination of raspberry coulis and apple juice. This is the perfect dinner party dessert, as all elements can be prepared in advance.

SEASON 5 · ANNIE & JASON

RASPBERRY AND WHITE CHOCOLATE CHEESECAKE
WITH CHOCOLATE SHARDS

PREP 45 MINS COOK 1 HOUR 30 MINS + 1 HOUR COOLING + 3 HOURS CHILLING SERVES 10

melted butter, to grease
200g digestive biscuits
85g butter, melted
600g *labneh*
150g caster sugar
½ tsp vanilla extract
4 large eggs
260g white chocolate, melted
300g sour cream

RASPBERRY SYRUP

1 tbsp caster sugar
175g fresh or frozen raspberries
60ml water
2 tsp cornflour dissolved in 1 tbsp cold water

CHOCOLATE SHARDS

25g macadamia nuts, toasted and coarsely chopped
100g caster sugar
50ml water
150g white chocolate

fresh raspberries, to serve

1 To make the raspberry syrup, stir the sugar, raspberries and water in a small saucepan over medium heat until soft. Stir in the cornflour mixture, then simmer until slightly thickened. Strain the syrup into a small jug, discarding the seeds. Refrigerate until cold.

2 Grease the base and sides of a 20cm springform pan with melted butter and line the base with baking paper. Process the biscuits in a food processor until fine crumbs form. Add the butter and process to combine. Press the mixture over the base of the prepared pan, then refrigerate until required.

3 Preheat the oven to 160°C. Using an electric mixer, beat the *labneh*, sugar and vanilla extract until smooth and the sugar has dissolved. Beat in the eggs, one at a time.

4 Fill a small saucepan one-third full with water and bring to a gentle simmer. Place the chocolate in a small heatproof bowl, place over the pan and stir until the chocolate has melted (don't let the bowl touch the water). Remove from the heat and whisk in the sour cream. Stir the chocolate mixture into the *labneh* mixture.

5 Pour half the mixture over the biscuit base. Drizzle with 2 tablespoons of raspberry syrup. Pour the remaining mixture on top. Pour the remaining syrup into a squeezy bottle. Starting from the centre of the cake, draw concentric circles with the syrup to the outside. Run a skewer from the centre to the edge of the cake to create a web effect.

6 Bake the cheesecake for 1¼ hours, or until almost set (the cheesecake should still have a slight wobble in the centre). Leave to cool in the oven for 1 hour with the door ajar, then refrigerate for 3 hours, or until set.

7 To make the chocolate shards, line two oven trays with baking paper. Spread the nuts in a single layer on one tray.

continued next page ➤

RASPBERRY AND WHITE CHOCOLATE CHEESECAKE

WITH CHOCOLATE SHARDS

(continued)

8 Stir the sugar and water in a medium-sized saucepan over medium heat, without boiling, until the sugar has dissolved, using a wet pastry brush to brush any stray grains on the inside of the pan back down into the mixture. Bring to the boil, then boil, uncovered and without stirring, for approximately 10 minutes, or until the mixture begins to turn golden brown. Pour the mixture over the nuts on the tray. Cool for 5 minutes or until set, then break into pieces and process in a food processor until coarse crumbs form.

9 Fill a small saucepan one-third full with water and bring to a gentle simmer. Place the chocolate in a small heatproof bowl, place over the pan and stir until the chocolate has melted (don't let the bowl touch the water). Thinly spread the chocolate onto the remaining prepared tray and sprinkle the praline in a thin layer on top. Set aside to cool and set, then break into shards.

10 Top the cheesecake with chocolate shards and raspberries. Drizzle the syrup on each plate before serving.

FRIED APPLE PIE
WITH SALTED CARAMEL

PREP 30 MINS + 30 MINS CHILLING COOK 40 MINS SERVES 4

200g crème fraîche
zest and juice of ½ lemon
100g caster sugar
2 tsp ground cinnamon
a pinch of salt
vegetable oil, for deep-frying

PASTRY

300g plain flour
20g cornflour
50g sugar
a pinch of salt
60g butter, softened
125ml water

APPLE FILLING

100g butter
4 Granny Smith apples, 2 peeled and roughly chopped, 2 peeled and finely diced
125ml apple juice
½ tsp ground cinnamon
1 vanilla bean, seeds scraped
55g brown sugar

PASTRY CRUMBS

100g plain flour
100g butter, chopped
50g caster sugar
1 tsp ground cinnamon
100g hazelnut meal

SALTED CARAMEL SAUCE

100g caster sugar
1 tbsp water
200ml thickened cream
salt, to taste

1 Combine the crème fraîche with the lemon zest and juice in a small bowl. Cover and refrigerate until needed.

2 Combine the sugar, cinnamon and salt in a small bowl and set aside.

3 To make the pastry, sift the flours, sugar and salt into the bowl of an electric mixer fitted with a dough hook. Add the butter and water and mix on low speed until a dough forms. Increase the speed to medium and mix for a further 3 minutes. Cover the dough in cling film and refrigerate for 30 minutes.

4 Meanwhile, to make the apple filling, melt half the butter in a medium frying pan over medium heat. Add the chopped apples and cook, stirring, for 2 minutes. Add the apple juice and half the cinnamon and simmer for a further 7 minutes, or until softened. Process the mixture in a food processor until a purée forms, then transfer to a medium bowl to cool.

5 Melt the remaining butter in a medium frying pan over medium heat. Add the diced apples, vanilla seeds, sugar and remaining cinnamon and cook, stirring, for 10 minutes, or until the apples are just tender. Stir the mixture into apple purée and allow to cool completely.

6 Roll out the dough between two sheets of baking paper until 2mm thick. Using a 10cm-round cutter, cut out 8 circles from the dough.

7 Divide the cooled apple mixture among the centre of 4 pastry rounds, leaving a 1cm border. Top with remaining pastry rounds and pinch the edges to seal.

8 Preheat the oven to 170°C. To make the pastry crumbs, place all the ingredients in the bowl of an electric mixer and beat on medium speed until well combined. Flatten out the dough on a baking paper-lined oven tray and bake for 12 minutes, or until crisp and golden. Cool completely, then process in a food processor until coarse crumbs form.

continued next page ➤

FRIED APPLE PIE
WITH SALTED CARAMEL
(continued)

9 To make the salted caramel, place the sugar and water in a small frying pan over medium heat and cook, without stirring, for 5 minutes, or until golden and the sugar has dissolved. Stir in the cream and cook for 1 minute, or until smooth. Remove from the heat and stir in the salt, to taste. Allow to cool in the fridge while you fry the pies.

10 Fill a deep-fryer or large saucepan one-third full with vegetable oil and heat over medium heat to 180°C (or until a cube of bread turns golden in 10 seconds). Gently drop the pies into the oil and fry, turning halfway, for 3 minutes, or until crisp and golden. Remove with a slotted spoon and drain on paper towel. Dust with cinnamon sugar.

11 Divide the fried apple pies among serving plates and drizzle over the warmed salted caramel sauce. Top with lemon crème fraîche, sprinkle with pastry crumbs and serve.

You could use any type of fresh fruit in this trifle – try strawberries and oranges, peaches and cherries or stewed apple and blackberries.

DEB'S TRIFLE

PREP 45 MINS COOK 1 HOUR 15 MINS + 4 HOURS CHILLING + 5 HOURS FREEZING SERVES 10

melted butter, to grease
125g raspberries
125g blueberries

CUSTARD AND ICE-CREAM

600ml cream
600ml milk
10 egg yolks
150g caster sugar
6 tsp cornflour
3 tsp vanilla extract

JELLY

300g raspberries
500ml clear apple juice
1 tbsp powdered gelatine

CAKE

200g butter, softened
220g caster sugar
2 eggs
300g self-raising flour
180ml milk

1 To make the custard and ice-cream, heat the cream and milk in a medium-sized saucepan until hot.

2 Whisk the remaining ingredients in a large bowl until combined. Slowly whisk in the hot cream mixture until combined. Return the mixture to the saucepan and stir over low–medium heat for 5 minutes, or until thickened. Strain using a fine sieve and divide into 2 bowls. Cover surface with cling film and refrigerate for 2 hours, or until cold.

3 Place one bowl of cooled custard into an ice-cream maker and churn according to the manufacturer's instructions. Transfer to an airtight container and freeze for 3 hours.

4 To make the jelly, place the raspberries and apple juice in a saucepan over medium heat. Stir with a wooden spoon, breaking down the raspberries, for 7 minutes, or until softened. Remove from the heat and strain through a sieve into a bowl, discarding the seeds. Sprinkle over the gelatine and stir until dissolved. Pour into a 18 x 20cm lined with cling film and refrigerate for 4 hours or overnight until set. When set, cut the jelly into 2cm cubes.

5 To make the cake, preheat the oven to 180°C. Grease a 20cm cake pan with melted butter and line the base and sides with baking paper. Using an electric mixer, beat the butter and sugar until light and fluffy. Beat in the eggs, one at time, then beat in the flour and milk in two batches. Pour the mixture into the prepared cake pan. Bake for 50 minutes, or until golden brown and a skewer inserted in the centre of the cake comes out clean. Stand in the pan for 5 minutes, then turn out onto a wire rack to cool completely. Cut into 2cm cubes.

6 To assemble the trifle, layer cake cubes, jelly, custard, berries and ice-cream into serving glasses and serve.

PETIT APPLE LATTICE PIES
WITH SPICED CRÈME ANGLAISE

PREP 1 HOUR   COOK 45 MINS + 30 MINS CHILLING   MAKES 12

APPLE FILLING

2kg large Granny Smith apples, peeled, cored and cut into 2cm pieces
440g caster sugar
½ tsp ground cinnamon
100ml water
90g butter
2 tbsp orange marmalade

PASTRY

melted butter, to grease
900g plain flour, sifted, plus extra, to dust
90g caster sugar
375g cold butter, chopped
a pinch of salt
3 egg yolks
½ tbsp lemon juice
125ml chilled water
60ml milk, to brush
raw sugar, to dust

SPICED CRÈME ANGLAISE

500ml full-cream milk
500ml pouring cream
2 tsp vanilla bean paste
1 cinnamon stick
1 star anise
8 egg yolks
275g caster sugar

double cream, to serve

1 To make the apple filling, place the apples, sugar, cinnamon and water in a large saucepan over medium heat and cook, stirring occasionally, for 4 minutes, or until the sugar has dissolved. Bring to the boil, then reduce the heat to low–medium. Cook, covered and stirring occasionally, for 15 minutes, or until the apples are tender. Drain slightly, leaving a little liquid in the pan, then stir in the butter and marmalade. Set aside to cool.

2 To make the pastry, preheat the oven to 180°C and grease 12 9cm-round fluted tart tins with removable bases with melted butter. Process the flour, sugar, butter and salt in a food processor until the mixture resembles crumbs. Add the egg yolks, lemon juice and water and process until the mixture just comes together. Shape into a disc, wrap in cling film and refrigerate for 30 minutes.

3 Using a floured rolling pin, roll out the pastry on a lightly floured work surface until 2–3mm thick. Using a 12cm-round cutter, cut out 12 rounds of pastry and ease the circles into the prepared tins. Roll out the remaining pastry and cut into 1cm strips.

4 Fill the pastry cases with the cold apple mixture. Place the pastry strips on top to form a lattice pattern and press the ends of the strips to join the pastry crust. Brush with a little milk and dust with sugar. Bake for 35 minutes, or until golden.

5 To make the crème anglaise, place the milk, cream, vanilla bean paste, cinnamon stick and star anise in a large, heavy-based saucepan over low heat and bring to a simmer, then remove from the heat.

6 In a separate bowl, whisk the egg yolks and sugar until combined. Gradually whisk the egg and sugar mixture into the hot milk mixture in the saucepan, then stir over low heat for about 8 minutes, or until thick enough to coat the back of a wooden spoon. Using a sieve, strain the mixture into a jug.

7 Divide the apple pies among serving plates and serve with crème anglaise and cream.

Crème anglaise is a French pouring custard with the consistency of thin cream – it can be served warm or cold.

SEASON 5 · BREE & JESSICA

CHOCOLATE RAVIOLI
WITH CHOCOLATE SAUCE AND ORANGE

PREP 20 MINS + 15 MINS RESTING   SERVES 4

150g mascarpone
1 tsp vanilla extract
1 tbsp icing sugar

FILLING

130g ricotta
1 tbsp orange-flavoured liqueur
2 tbsp finely grated dark chocolate (70% cocoa)
1 tsp orange zest
1 tbsp icing sugar

CHOCOLATE PASTA

335g Italian '00' pasta flour, plus extra, to dust
50g cocoa powder
3 tbsp caster sugar
4 eggs

CHOCOLATE SAUCE

300ml thickened cream
100g dark chocolate (70% cocoa), finely chopped
1 tbsp brown sugar
2 tbsp orange-flavoured liqueur

CANDIED ORANGE ZEST

2 oranges, zest peeled into thin strips
75g caster sugar
2 tbsp orange-flavoured liqueur

orange segments, to serve

1 To make the filling, combine all the ingredients in a small bowl. Cover and set aside until needed.

2 To make the pasta, sift the flour, cocoa powder and sugar into a bowl. Add the eggs and 1 tablespoon chilled water and mix to combine. Turn out the dough onto a lightly floured work surface and knead for 4 minutes, or until smooth and the dough just comes together. Set aside for 15 minutes to rest. Using a rolling pin, flatten the dough until 5mm thick and about 12cm wide – nearly the width of your pasta machine. Set your pasta machine at its widest setting, then feed the dough through, narrowing the settings on your machine one notch at a time until you reach the thinnest setting.

3 Using a 6cm-round cutter, cut out 24 rounds from the dough. Place 1 teaspoon of filling in the centre of half the dough circles. Moisten the edges with water, then top with the remaining dough circles and press the edges to seal.

4 To make the chocolate sauce, place the cream in a small saucepan over low heat and stir until almost boiling. Place the chocolate in a medium bowl and pour over the hot cream. Stand for 5 minutes, then add the sugar and liqueur. Stir until smooth and combined.

5 To make the candied orange zest, place all the ingredients with 80ml water in a small, non-stick frying pan over medium heat. Bring to the boil and cook until it becomes a golden toffee. Place separated on a cooling rack until dry and set.

6 Place the mascarpone, vanilla extract and sugar in a small bowl and stir to combine.

7 Cook the ravioli in small batches in a large saucepan of boiling water for 2 minutes, or until they rise to the top. Remove with a slotted spoon and drain on paper towel.

8 Divide the ravioli among 4 plates. Top with candied orange zest and spoon over the chocolate sauce. Serve with orange segments and mascarpone.

STRAWBERRY CHAMPAGNE TRIFLE

PREP 50 MINS + SETTING COOK 50 MINS SERVES 4–6

80g strawberries, chopped (for coulis)
4 large strawberries, sliced (to macerate)
2 tbsp freeze-dried strawberries, crushed
double cream, to serve

JELLY

6 sheets gold-strength leaf gelatine
325ml Champagne
80g caster sugar
175g strawberries, hulled and thinly sliced

CUSTARD CAKE

500ml warm milk
1 vanilla bean, seeds scraped
4 eggs, separated
150g icing sugar
125g unsalted butter, melted
1 tbsp water
75g self-raising flour

SYRUP

80ml Champagne
1½ tbsp icing sugar
finely grated zest of ½ orange

SHORTBREAD CRUMB

80g salted butter
40g caster sugar
100g plain flour
25g rice flour

1 To make the jelly, line a 20cm x 15cm slice pan with cling film. Soak the gelatine sheets in a bowl of cold water for 5 minutes, or until soft.

2 Stir the Champagne and sugar over low heat, without boiling, until the sugar has dissolved. Remove from the heat. Squeeze excess water out of the gelatine and add to the Champagne mixture. Stir until dissolved. Pour into the prepared pan and scatter over the sliced strawberries. Refrigerate for several hours or overnight until set. Invert onto a chopping board and cut into 6cm rounds.

3 To make the cake, preheat the oven to 160°C. Grease a 20cm square cake pan and line the base and sides with baking paper. Stir the milk and vanilla seeds in a saucepan over low heat until hot. Remove from the heat and set aside to cool and infuse.

4 Beat the egg whites until soft peaks form and set aside. Beat the egg yolks and sugar until light and creamy. Slowly pour in the butter and water, beating to combine. Slowly pour in the cooled milk mixture, beating to combine. Whisk in the flour, then fold in the egg whites. Pour the mixture into the prepared pan. Bake for 40–45 minutes, or until the top is golden and a skewer comes out clean once inserted. Cool in the pan. Once cooled, invert onto a chopping board and cut out 4 circles using a 6cm-round cutter.

5 To make the syrup, stir the Champagne, sugar and zest in a small saucepan until the sugar has dissolved. Cool for 5 minutes, then strain.

6 Place half the syrup in a saucepan and add the chopped strawberries. Cook over medium heat, stirring, for 3 minutes. Transfer to a blender and blend until smooth, then strain through a fine sieve to make a coulis. Pour the remaining syrup over the sliced strawberries in a single layer. Set aside to macerate.

7 To make the shortbread crumb, beat the butter and sugar with an electric mixer until pale and creamy. Stir in the flour until just combined to form a smooth dough. Roll between two pieces of baking paper until 2mm thick.

8 Bake for 15 minutes, or until golden and crisp. Cool completely, then crush to form coarse crumbs. Stir through the freeze-dried strawberries until well combined.

9 To assemble, layer serving dishes with jelly, cake and cream and serve with the crumb mixture, coulis and macerated strawberries on the side.

Freeze-dried strawberries are available from delicatessens and specialist grocers. You can be inventive in the way you present this dish by varying the shapes and sizes of the cake and jelly. You can also try replacing strawberries with raspberries.

Rough puff pastry can be tricky to work with as you have to work very quickly. Keeping the pastry as cold as possible will make it more manageable.

PEACH AND APRICOT TARTE TATIN
WITH CINNAMON ICE-CREAM

PREP 1 HOUR + CHURNING/FREEZING COOK 1 HOUR SERVES 4

110g caster sugar
125ml water
2 large firm ripe peaches, peeled and cut into 2cm dice
4 firm ripe apricots, peeled and cut into 2cm dice
60g butter, cut into 5mm dice

CINNAMON ICE-CREAM

500ml thickened cream
250ml milk
1 cinnamon stick, broken
1 vanilla bean, seeds scraped
6 egg yolks
150g caster sugar

THYME AND CINNAMON SYRUP

55g caster sugar
60ml water
¼ bunch thyme
½ cinnamon stick, broken

'ROUGH' PUFF PASTRY

200g plain flour
200g cold butter, chopped
80ml ice-cold water
a pinch of salt

1 To make the ice-cream, stir the cream, milk, cinnamon, vanilla bean and seeds in a saucepan over low heat until hot. Remove from the heat. Set aside for 30 minutes to infuse.

2 Whisk the egg yolks and sugar until pale and creamy. Slowly add the strained cream mixture, whisking continuously. Return the mixture to the saucepan and stir over low heat until thick enough to coat the back of a wooden spoon. Strain, allow to cool then refrigerate until cold. Churn in an ice-cream maker according to manufacturer's instructions.

3 To make the thyme and cinnamon syrup, stir all the ingredients in a small saucepan over medium heat until the sugar has dissolved and the syrup thickens. Set aside to infuse and cool. Strain.

4 To make the pastry, pulse the flour and butter in a food processor five or six times until mixture is rough with large chunks of butter through it. Working very quickly, turn the processor back on, add the water and after 2 seconds turn it off. The mixture should still be rough and flecked with butter. Turn out onto a floured surface and knead for 30 seconds to bring the dough together. Shape into a rectangle, wrap in cling film and refrigerate for 30 minutes.

5 Roll out the pastry between two sheets of baking paper into a 30cm x 15cm rectangle about 1½ cm thick (you will be able to see streaks of butter). Fold into thirds from the short end. Wrap in cling film and refrigerate for 30 minutes. Repeat the rolling, folding and resting in the refrigerator twice.

6 Grease four 8cm-round (base measurement) pie tins. Line the bases with baking paper.

7 To make the caramel for the *tartes tatin*, stir the sugar and the water in a small, heavy-based saucepan over medium heat, without boiling, until the sugar has dissolved. Use a wet pastry brush to brush any stray grains on the inside of the pan back down into the mixture. Bring to the boil and boil, uncovered, without stirring, for 10–15 minutes, or until the mixture begins to turn light golden brown. Pour the caramel evenly into the pie tins.

continued next page ➤

PEACH AND APRICOT TARTE TATIN

WITH CINNAMON ICE-CREAM

(continued)

8 Divide the fruit among the tins and top with butter.

9 Roll out the pastry until 5mm thick. Cut out 4 circles just large enough to extend to the rims of the pie tins. Lay the circles over the top, lightly tucking in the edge around the fruit. Refrigerate for 30 minutes.

10 Meanwhile, preheat the oven to 200°C. Bake the *tartes* for 20–25 minutes, or until the pastry is crisp, golden and puffed.

11 Invert the *tartes tatin* onto serving plates and remove the baking paper. Serve with the ice-cream and drizzle with syrup.

DECONSTRUCTED CHOCOLATE AND RHUBARB TART

PREP 1 HOUR + FREEZING   COOK 1 HOUR 20 MINS   SERVES 4–6

BRAISED RHUBARB

1 bunch rhubarb, trimmed and cut into 3cm lengths
100g caster sugar
1 tbsp water
1 vanilla bean, seeds scraped

ICE-CREAM

300ml milk
300ml thickened cream
1 vanilla bean, seeds scraped
5 egg yolks
2 tsp vanilla extract
150g caster sugar

CHOCOLATE PASTRY

200g plain flour
2 tbsp caster sugar
35g Dutch cocoa powder
170g butter, chilled and cubed
1 tbsp cold water

GANACHE

300g dark chocolate (70% cocoa), chopped
125ml thickened cream
2 tbsp caster sugar

TUILES

1 egg white
55g caster sugar
35g plain flour
30g melted butter

HAZELNUT BISCUIT CRUMB

75g plain flour
10g cold butter, chopped
2 tbsp caster sugar
55g ground hazelnuts

1 To make the braised rhubarb, place all the ingredients in a medium-sized saucepan over low heat and cook, covered, for 5 minutes. Uncover and cook, stirring occasionally, for 10 to 15 minutes, or until tender. Allow to cool, then refrigerate until cold.

2 To make the ice-cream, stir the milk, cream, vanilla bean and seeds in a saucepan over medium heat until hot. Remove from the heat and allow to cool slightly. Whisk the egg yolks, extract and sugar until pale and creamy. Slowly add the hot milk mixture, whisking continuously. Return the mixture to the saucepan and stir over low heat for 10–15 minutes, or until thick enough to coat the back of a wooden spoon. Strain then allow to cool and refrigerate until cold. Churn in an ice-cream maker according to the manufacturer's instructions. Transfer the soft ice-cream to a shallow dish and swirl through 250ml of the cooled braised rhubarb. Freeze.

3 To make the chocolate pastry, process the flour, sugar, cocoa and butter until the mixture resembles coarse crumbs. Slowly add the water until the mixture just comes together to form a dough. Turn out onto a lightly floured surface and shape into a disc. Wrap in cling film and refrigerate for 1 hour.

4 Preheat the oven to 180°C. Line an oven tray with baking paper. Roll out the dough between 2 sheets of baking paper until 2mm thick. Cut into small rectangles (about 8cm x 4cm). Place on the prepared tray and bake for 15–20 minutes, or until cooked and crisped. Transfer to a wire rack to cool.

continued next page ➤

DECONSTRUCTED CHOCOLATE AND RHUBARB TART
(continued)

5 To make the ganache, place the chocolate in a heatproof bowl. Stir the cream and sugar in a small saucepan over low heat until the sugar has dissolved and the mixture is hot. Pour over the chocolate and stand for 5 minutes. Stir until smooth and combined. Pour into a shallow container and refrigerate until firm.

6 To make the tuiles, preheat the oven to 180°C and line an oven tray with baking paper. Whisk the egg white and sugar in a bowl until frothy. Stir in remaining ingredients to form a paste. Spread the paste onto the tray to form 8cm x 3cm oval shapes. Bake for 5–6 minutes or until golden.

7 To make the biscuit crumb, line an oven tray with baking paper. Rub the flour into the butter and sugar until the mixture resembles coarse crumbs. Mix in the hazelnuts and spread onto the prepared tray. Bake for 8–10 minutes, or until golden. Cool on the tray.

8 Serve the ice-cream, chocolate pastry, tuiles and braised rhubarb with the hazelnut crumb and spoonfuls of ganache.

If you don't have an ice-cream machine, transfer the mixture to a shallow container. Freeze until frozen at the edges. Beat with an electric mixer, then return to the freezer. Repeat this process three times.

Leftover biscuits will keep in an airtight container for up to three days. Alternatively, only bake four of the biscuits and freeze uncooked biscuits to bake for another occasion.

PEACHES AND CREAM

PREP 1 HOUR + FREEZING TIME COOK 35 MINS SERVES 4

500ml peach juice

CRÈME FRAÎCHE ICE-CREAM
200ml milk
175g icing sugar
600g crème fraîche
finely grated zest of 1 lemon
1 tsp vanilla extract

FENNEL BISCUITS
135g spelt wholemeal flour
115g rolled oats
55g dark brown sugar
110g butter
20g coconut oil
2 tsp fennel seeds
1 tsp baking power
a pinch of salt

ROASTED PEACHES
4 firm ripe yellow peaches, halved
20g butter, melted
1½ tbsp brown sugar
½ bunch lemon thyme

VANILLA CREAM
150ml thickened cream
1 tsp vanilla bean paste
1 tbsp icing sugar

micro herbs, to decorate

1 To make the ice-cream, whisk the milk and sugar in a bowl until the sugar has dissolved. Stir in the remaining ingredients. Churn in an ice-cream maker according to the manufacturer's instructions.

2 To make the biscuits, process all the ingredients to form a dough. Turn onto a lightly floured surface and shape into a disc. Wrap in cling film and refrigerate for 15 minutes.

3 Preheat the oven to 180°C. Line an oven tray with baking paper. Roll out the dough between two sheets of baking paper until 3mm thick. Cut out 8cm rounds using a cookie cutter. Place on the prepared tray 3cm apart and bake for 15 minutes, or until golden and crisp. Transfer to a wire rack to cool.

4 Place the peach juice in a saucepan over medium heat and simmer until reduced to a syrup consistency. Cool completely.

5 Increase the oven temperature to 200°C. To roast the peaches, brush them all over with butter and sprinkle with sugar. Place in a flameproof roasting dish, in a single layer, cut-side down. Sprinkle with sprigs of lemon thyme and roast for 15–20 minutes, or until tender. Remove from the dish and peel away the skins. Cool completely.

6 To make the vanilla cream, beat all ingredients together until soft peaks form.

7 To assemble, place a biscuit on each plate. Top with one peach half. Spoon or pipe the vanilla cream into the centre. Top with the remaining peach half. Sprinkle with micro herbs and serve with the ice-cream and peach syrup.

INDEX

A

agedashi tofu 20
aioli, chilli lime 31
apple
- filling 210
- pie, fried 205–206

apricot
- peach and apricot tarte tatin 217–218

asparagus and pea risotto 85
avocado
- cream 7–8
- mousse 150
- purée 43

B

bacon huevos rancheros 35
baguettes, Vietnamese 36
balsamic glaze 51
banana
- caramelised 181–182
- tartlets 181–182

beef
- baharat beef 103
- beef sukiyaki 82
- cheeks 153
- Chinese braised beef ribs 142
- massaman curry 93–94
- wagyu beef carpaccio 40

beetroot
- carpaccio 52
- pomegranate and redcurrant vinaigrette 24
- tart 47

blackberry chutney 9–10
blueberry
- coulis 178
- toffee blueberries 178

brandy pâté, Grandma's 9–10
breads
- brioche cup 178
- brioche rolls 9–10
- buns 48
- crusty bread 23, 67
- damper, breakfast 15
- flat bread 100
- lavosh 149
- pizza dough 51
- roti 93–94

brioche rolls 9–10
broth 4
butter, sage 59

C

chicken
- chicken adobo tortillas 39
- crispy 27
- hainan chicken 107
- Japanese-inspired poached chicken 118
- jerk chicken 95–96
- livers with port and prosciutto 67
- nasi goreng 104
- prosciutto-wrapped chicken 89

chimichurri 39
chocolate
- cake 197–198
- chocolate almond praline 187–188
- chocolate and rhubarb tart, deconstructed 219–220
- chocolate hazelnut cake 187–188
- chocolate raspberry macarons 189–190
- ganache 183–184, 199–200
- mousse 187–188, 189–190, 197–198
- mousse cake 170
- pastry 219–220
- raspberry and white chocolate cheesecake 203–204
- ravioli 213
- sauce 172, 213
- shards 203–204

chutney
- blackberry 9–10
- spiced mango 122

cookies
- sesame and cinnamon 174

cream
- avocado 7–8
- buttercream 183
- caramel 187–188
- crème de menthe 197–198
- lime and dill 68
- pastry 181–182
- spiced crème anglaise 210
- vanilla 223

croquettes, goat's cheese 44
croutons, goat's cheese 12

curry
massaman 93–94
sauce 154
custard and ice-cream 209
custard cake 214

D
damper, breakfast 15
dates, spiced coffee-soaked 174
dessert
apple lattice pies, petit 210
apple pie, fried 205–206
banana tartlets 181–182
blueberry brioche cup 178
chocolate and rhubarb tart, deconstructed 219–220
chocolate hazelnut cake 187–188
chocolate mousse cake 170
chocolate peppermint delice 197–198
chocolate raspberry pop delight 189–190
chocolate ravioli 213
dates, spiced coffee-soaked 174
doughnuts, Italian potato 173
figs, sake 177
gorgonzola soufflés, twice baked 169
macarons 183–184
peach and apricot tarte tatin 217–218
peaches and cream 223
raspberry and white chocolate cheesecake 203–204
red velvet with chocolate and raspberries 199–200
strawberry and amaretto semifreddo 194
strawberry champagne trifle 214
trifle, Deb's 209
yoghurt pannacotta 193
zeppole 173
dressing 27, 31, 63, 74, 117, 125
coleslaw 138
mentsuyu 78
nam jim 141
duck
confit duck leg 163
warm duck salad 24
tea-smoked duck 146

E
egg, Scotch 56

F
fennel biscuits 223
feta, baked 149
figs, sake 177
filling, macaron 189–190
flavouring
blueberry 183–184
mango 183–184
pistachio 183–184
fondant, mint 197–198
fritters
corn, zucchini and haloumi 7–8

G
ganache 187–188, 199–200, 219–220
goat's cheese
croquettes 44
croutons 12
mousse 47
gremolata, green olive 133
gyoza, pork 20

H
hazelnut biscuit crumb 219–220
honey, rosemary 149

I
ice-cream 219–220
cinnamon 217–218
crème fraîche 223

J
jam, cherry 187–188
jambalaya, cajun 90
jelly 209, 214
lemon 193
raspberry 199–200

K
kangaroo, spiced 122

L
labneh 178
lamb
feta, beetroot and rosemary honey, with 149
rack 133
roulade 111–112

lemon
curd 183–184
jelly 193

M
macadamias, caramelised 44
macarons 183–184
chocolate raspberry 189–190
mayonnaise 28, 36, 40, 145
herb 56
moussaka, baked 121
mousse
avocado 150
goat's cheese 47
mushroom
mushrooms and Chinese greens 19
ravioli in porcini broth 55
soup 12

N
nasi goreng 104
noodles 4
vermicelli 19

O
oil, garlic ginger 99
orange zest, candied 213

P
pancake batter 32
pasta
mushroom ravioli in porcini broth 55
pasta with chorizo and pesto 100
pumpkin ravioli 59
paste
green curry 117
red curry 60
rempah 48
yellow curry 154
pastry 47, 181–182, 205–206, 210
chocolate 219–220
cream 181–182
crostoli 194
crumbs 205–206
'rough' puff 217–218
pâté
Grandma's brandy 9–10
peach
peach and apricot tarte tatin 217–218
roasted peaches 223
pear
caramelised 169
poached 170
purée 138
peppermint crumble 197–198
pesto 100
mint 111–112
pizza with pear, pancetta and rocket 51
pork
cheek 129–130
fillet 138
gyoza 20
patties 36
poached pork belly 108
pork and fennel sausages, handmade Sicilian 74
pork and prawn pancakes, Vietnamese 32
prosciutto, apple and gorgonzola pork chops 85
ribs, Mexican 137
praline
chocolate almond 187–188
hazelnut 187–188
macadamia 181–182
prawns *see* seafood
pumpkin ravioli 59

Q
quail with corn and jus 157

R
raspberry
chocolate raspberry macarons 189–190
coulis 183–184, 189–190, 199–200
jelly 199–200
mousse 189–190
raspberry and white chocolate cheesecake 203–204
syrup 203–204
relish
tomato, smokey 7–8
rice
coconut 95–96
lemon 134
risotto
asparagus and pea 85
scampi 126
rösti stack, zucchini and potato 71

S
salad
apple and mango 141
Asian rice noodle 27
baby leaf 149
beetroot and freekeh 125
cabbage 150

coleslaw 39
warm duck 24
Greek 121
green papaya 63
kachumber 122
orange and fennel slaw 138
pickled 93–94
pomegranate and lime 39
prawn, zesty 31
rocket and apple 44
Vietnamese 117
salsa
bloody Mary 35
pineapple 95–96
salsa verde 137
salt curing mixture 52
sauce
agedashi 20
apple cider jus 129–130
beurre rouge 86
black olive 114
brandy 108
cheese 121
chilli, fresh 107
chilli soy dipping sauce 16
chocolate 172
cranberry 146
dipping 32
ginger spring onion oil 107
horseradish cream 52
jus 89, 157
mint yoghurt 103
nuoc cham 107
parsley and anchovy 81
peanut and lime dipping sauce 60
salted caramel 205–206
spicy tomato 15
tahini yoghurt 125
XO 19
yoghurt 95–96
seafood
barramundi, crispy 141
beetroot carpaccio with cured salmon 52
bisque 145
blue-eye trevalla, pan-fried 81
chilli soft shell crab, Singaporean 48
crab congee 99
fresh fish fingers 78
hapuku with black olive sauce 114
keralan fish moilee 134
kingfish, cured 154
Moreton Bay bugs 145
mulloway 86
oysters, steamed 19
pork and prawn pancakes, Vietnamese 32
prawn cakes 60
prawn salad, zesty 31
prawns, avocado and pink grapefruit 68
prawns, saganaki 23
red mullet 158–160
salmon, confit 150
salmon, cured 28
salmon fish fingers 78
salmon, pan-seared 125
salt and pepper mud crab 16
salt and pepper prawns 63
scallop ceviche 43
scampi, grilled 64
scampi risotto 126
swordfish, grilled 77
swordfish, pan-seared 117
tuna, seared Moroccan 28
seasoning, adobo 39
shortbread crumb 214
soup
broth 4
consommé 99
mushroom 12
mushroom broth 118
seafood bisque 145
sukiyaki broth 82
spice
mix 90
rub 122
stock
beef 82
dashi 82
fish 126
lamb 111–112
strawberry
gelée 194
macerated strawberries 194
strawberry and amaretto semifreddo 194
strawberry champagne trifle 214
syrup
amaretto 194
raspberry 203–204
red wine syrup 153
thyme 193
thyme and cinnamon 217–218

T

tart
banana tartlets 181–182

beetroot 47
chocolate and rhubarb tart, deconstructed 219–220
peach and apricot tarte tatin 217–218
tofu, agedashi 20
tomato relish 7–8, 15
topping
almond 178
tortillas
bacon huevos rancheros 35
chicken adobo tortillas 39
tuiles 219–220
turkey san choi bow 3

V

vegetables
artichoke purée 158–160
artichokes, hay-smoked 158–160
beans, sambal 64
beetroot, honey-glazed 165
beetroot, roasted 149
beetroot reduction 165
carrots, pickled 78
cauliflower purée 161–162
celeriac purée 86, 153
celeriac *remoulade* 145
corn purée 157
eggplant marinade 77
fennel, caramelised 81
fennel, roasted 150
fennel purée 146
garam masala potatoes 122
garlic mash 89
leek mash 74
mushrooms 161–162
mushrooms and Chinese greens 19
onions, caramelised 51
onions, pickled 137
pickled 36, 153
pommes dauphine 133
popcorn 157
potato croquettes 129–130
potato doughnuts, Italian 173
potato rösti 138
prosciutto-wrapped asparagus 7–8
pumpkin purée 108
purple carrots 158–160
radish, pickled 161–162
rhubarb, braised 219–220
sweet potato mash 103
tomatoes, roasted 74, 103
veggie chips 114
vermicelli noodles 19
vinaigrette
beetroot, pomegranate and redcurrant 24

W

watermelon, compressed 165

X

XO sauce 19

Z

zucchini and potato rösti stack 71

hachette
AUSTRALIA

Published in Australia and New Zealand in 2015
by Hachette Australia
(an imprint of Hachette Australia Pty Limited)
Level 17, 207 Kent Street, Sydney NSW 2000
www.hachette.com.au

10 9 8 7 6 5 4 3 2 1

National Library of Australia
Cataloguing-in-Publication data:

MKR: best of the best cookbook.

978 0 7336 3475 8 (paperback)

Cooking.

641.5

Cover design and internal design by Liz Seymour/Seymour Designs
Photography by Alan Benson
Food styling by Trish Heagerty
Food preparation by Tracey Meharg
Typeset in 10/12 pt Conduit light ITC by Seymour Designs
Printed in China by 1010 Printing International